The Ultimate Breakfast Sandwich Maker Cookbook

100 Delicious, Energizing and Simple Breakfast Recipes

LEGAL DISCLAIMER

The information contained in this book is the opinion of the author and is based on the author's personal experience and observations. The author does not assume any liability whatsoever for the use of or inability to use any or all information contained in this book, and accepts no responsibility for any loss or damages of any kind that may be incurred by the reader as a result of actions arising from the use of information in this book. Use this information at your own risk. The author reserves the right to make any changes he or she deems necessary to future versions of the publication to ensure its accuracy.

It's a fact: readers who follow an ACTION GUIDE as they read and use cookbooks tend to have the most success!

Here's what I'm going to do to thank you for downloading my book. Go to the link below to instantly sign up for these bonuses.

Here's just a taste of what subscribers get:

Printable Kitchen Guides:

- Keep your food fresher for longer with the Extra-Long Food Storage Guide
- No more guess work in the kitchen -- Metric Conversion Guide
- Make delicious spreads in minutes -- Easy Spreads Guide
- Protect your family from consuming undercooked meat -- Meat Grilling Guide
- Many more new upcoming high-quality guides

Books and Recipes:

- New mouth-watering recipes you have NEVER tried before
- New books I publish for FREE

GRAB YOUR FREEBIES NOW AT
COOKINGWITHAFOODIE.COM

TABLE OF CONTENTS

Introduction 8
    The Importance of Breakfast 9
    The Problems with Making a Quick and Healthy Breakfast 9
    Recipes with Minimal Steps and Easy Preparation 9
    No Mess and Quick Clean-Up! 10
    Fun, Healthy, and Easy-to-Make Recipes 10
    Variety of Recipes 10

Tips and Techniques 11
    Cutting Down on Preparation Time 12
    Handy Guide to Food Storage and Safety 17
    Tips for Safe Storage of Perishable, Semi-Perishable, & Non-Perishable Foods 20

Recipes 23
    I. Traditional Breakfast Egg & Omelette Sandwiches 24
        Classic Sausage, Egg, & Cheddar English Muffin Sandwich 25
        Classic Smoked Ham, Egg, & Havarti Bagel Sandwich 26
        Classic Bacon, Scrambled Egg, & Cheddar Biscuit 27
        Classic Sausage, Mozzarella, & Cinnamon-Sugar Waffle Sandwich 28
        Classic Bacon, Tomato, and Pesto Cream Cheese Bagel Sandwich 29
        Savory Sausage, Goat Cheese, & Garlic Cream Cheese English Muffin Sandwich 30
        Classic Bacon, Scrambled Egg, & Maple Butter Waffle Sandwich 31
        Classic Smoked Ham, Scrambled Egg, & Swiss Biscuit Sandwich 32

Sweet & Savory Sausage, Egg, and Apple Pancake Sandwich 33

Caprese Bacon, Tomato, Mozzarella, & Fresh Basil English Muffin Sandwich 34

Hearty Bacon, Sausage, Crumbled Bleu Cheese, & Maple Aioli Bagel Sandwich. 35

Spicy Pepper Jack, Mozzarella, Avocado, & Fried Egg Biscuit Sandwich (Vegetarian) . . 36

Classic Sausage, Egg, & Cinnamon-Sugar Butter Pancake Sandwich. 37

II. Famous Breakfast Sandwiches 38

Spicy Chorizo, Egg, & Goat Cheese on a French Baguette 39

Bacon, Scrambled Egg, Tomato, & Herb Cream Cheese Bagel Sandwich 40

Fried Bologna, White Cheddar, & Spicy Mustard on a French Baguette 41

Santa Fe Omelette & Cheddar English Muffin Sandwich (Vegetarian) 42

Glazed Maple & Brown Sugar Sausage with Brie Pancake Sandwich 43

Bacon, Sharp Cheddar, and Fried Potato Biscuit Sandwich 44

New York Style" Everything" Bagel Sandwich 45

III. Chicken and Turkey Sandwiches 46

Roasted Turkey Breast, Sharp Cheddar, & Cranberry Biscuit Sandwich 47

Roasted Turkey Breast, Spinach, & Sun-Dried Cream Cheese Bagel Sandwich 48

Roasted Turkey Breast, Avocado Creme, & Provolone on a French Baguette. 49

Roasted Turkey Breast, Bacon, & Chipotle Aioli Biscuit Sandwich 50

Melty Mozzarella & BBQ Chicken on a French Baguette 51

Spicy Turkey Breast, Jalapeno, & Fresh Tomato Sourdough Melt. 52

Buffalo Chicken and Bleu Cheese on Sourdough 53

Roasted Turkey Breast, Bacon, & Apple Club on CInnamon-Raisin Bread. 54

Chicken Breast, Apple Jelly, & Mozzarella Walnut Bread Sandwich. 55

Chicken Breast, Fig Compote, & Brie English Muffin Sandwich 56

Chicken Breast, Pepperoni, and Parmesan on a French Baguette 57

IV. Bacon and Pork Sandwiches 58

Smoked Ham, Brie, & Honey Biscuit Sandwich 59

Smoked Ham, Gouda, & Blackberry Jam Waffle Sandwich 60

Bacon, Fresh Peach, & Mozzarella Melt on Wheat 61

Chorizo, Grilled Peppers, & Mozzarella English Muffin Sandwich 62

Pork Tenderloin, Apple, and White Cheddar on a French Baguette 63

Smoked Ham, Pear, & Brie on a Croissant 64

Hawaiian Pork Tenderloin & Fresh Pineapple on a Soft Roll 65

V. Beef Sandwiches 66

Shaved Steak, White Cheddar, & Caramelized Onion Sourdough Melt 67

Meatball Marinara with Goat Cheese & Mozzarella on a French Baguette 68

Roast Beef, Provolone, & Horseradish Aioli on a Soft Roll 69

Shaved Steak, White Cheddar, & BBQ Aioli Bagel Sandwich 70

VI. Calorie-Conscious 71

Roasted Turkey Breast, Asparagus, & Honey Goat Cheese on Wheat 72

Sharp Cheddar, Apple, & Spicy Horseradish Mustard on Wheat (Vegetarian) 73

Peach, Mozzarella, & Basil Pesto Greek Yogurt English Muffin Sandwich (Vegetarian) . 74

Mediterranean Feta, Spinach, & Sun-Dried Tomato on Pita (Vegetarian) 75

Turkey Bacon, Sauteed Veggies, and Goat Cheese on Pita 76

Roasted Turkey Breast, Parmesan, and Basil Pesto Aioli on Wheat 77

Pan-Fried Tofu, Spinach, and Honey Ricotta on a French Baguette (Vegetarian) 78

Sauteed Kale & Garlic with Havarti Melt on Wheat (Vegetarian) 79

Turkey Bacon, Avocado, & White Cheddar Wheat Melt 80

Roasted Turkey Breast, Artichoke, & Sun-Dried Tomato Greek Yogurt on Pita 81

Veggie Sausage, Soy Cheese, and Cherry Preserves English Muffin Sandwich (Vegan) .. 82

Veggie Bacon, Pan-Fried Tofu, & Soy Cheese Melt on Wheat (Vegan) 83

VII. Gluten-Free 84

Spicy Egg Salad, Bacon, and Tomato on Gluten-Free Bread 85

Smoked Ham, Swiss Cheese, & Raspberry Preserve Gluten-Free English
Muffin Sandwich 86

DIll Cream Cheese, Avocado, & Tomato Gluten-Free Bagel Sandwich (Vegetarian) 87

Huevos Rancheros Gluten-Free English Muffin Sandwich (Vegetarian) 88

Honey, Goat Cheese, & Fig Compote on Gluten-Free Cinnamon-Raisin
Bread (Vegetarian) 89

Bacon, Bleu Cheese, & Sauteed Baby Bella Mushrooms on Gluten-Free English Muffin .. 90

Sauteed Pepper, Havarti, and Scrambled Egg Gluten-Free Wheat
Sandwich (Vegetarian) 91

VIII. International Sandwiches 92

Spicy Mac n' Cheese, Jalapeno, & Bacon Melt on Sourdough 93

Italian Mozzarella Melt on a French Baguette 94

Italian Florentine English Muffin Breakfast Sandwich (Vegetarian) 95

Parisian Smoked Ham, Pear, & Havarti on a French Baguette 96

Cuban Medianoche on a Kaiser Roll 97

Chilean Chacarero on a Kaiser Roll 98

English Chip Butty English Muffin Sandwich 99

Canadian Roast Beef and Mustard on Rye 100

South African Gatsby on a French Baguette 101

Austrian Bosna Wurst on a Kaiser Roll 102

Malaysian Roti John on a French Baguette 103

Finnish Porilainen on Sourdough 104

Trinidadian Chickpea Double on Pita (Vegetarian) 105

Vietnamese Bahn Mi on a French Baguette 106

Irish Corned Beef Reuben on Rye 107

IX. Kid-Friendly 108

Tuna Salad, Granny Smith Apple, & American Cheese on White 109

Sloppy Joes with White Cheddar on a Hamburger Bun 110

Sliced Chicken Breast, Broccoli, & Cheddar on White 111

Roasted Turkey Breast, Marinara, & Mozzarella on a Hamburger Bun 112

Sliced Apple, Bacon, Honey, Butter on a French Baguette 113

Crunch Peanut Butter, Strawberry, & Brie Biscuit Sandwich (Vegetarian) 114

Honey-Glazed Ham, Grape Jelly, & Provolone Waffle Sandwich 115

Classic Peanut Butter & Jelly Bagel Sandwich (Vegan) 116

Cheddar, American, & Pickles Grilled Cheese on Wheat (Vegetarian) 117

Fruity Chicken Salad & Potato Chips on White 118

X. Brunch 119

Caramelized Apple, Brie, & Bacon on Sourdough 120

Maple Sausage, Strawberry Jam, & Nutella French Toast Sandwich 121

Caramelized Pear, Berry Cream Cheese, and Honey-Glazed Ham French Toast Sandwich 122

Sliced Chicken Breast, Goat Cheese, & Raspberry Jam English Muffin Sandwich 123

Caprese Waffle Sandwich with Sweet Balsamic Glaze (Vegetarian) 124

Sweet Lemon Cream Cheese and Fresh Berry Waffle Sandwich (Vegetarian) 125

Monte Cristo French Toast Sandwich with Fresh Strawberries 126

XI. Breakfast Sides 127
    Simple Roasted Breakfast Potatoes 128
    Simple Hash Brown "Casserole" 129
    Savory Sauteed Brussel Sprouts & Bacon 130
    Citrus & Avocado Arugula Salad 131
    Simple Potato Latkes 132
    Sauteed Green Beans with Bacon & Onion 133
    Classic Pan-Fried Home Fries 134
    Citrus, Honey, and Toasted Coconut Salad 135
    Super Simple Frozen Fruit Salad 136

XII. Dessert 137
    Fresh Strawberry, Banana, and Nutella Waffle Sandwich 138
    Dark Chocolate 'S'mores Cinnamon Swirl Sandwich 139
    Peanut Butter, Bacon, & Dark Chocolate Croissant Sandwich ... 140
    Granny Smith Apple & Honey Goat Cheese on Sugar-Encrusted Cinnamon Raisin Bread 141
    Chocolate & Brie Melt on Sourdough 142
    Bacon, Banana, & Nutella on Sugar-Encrusted Cinnamon Raisin Bread ... 143

Introduction

The Importance of Breakfast

Believe it or not, it's true: a healthy, hearty breakfast is truly the most important meal of the day. With the help of this book and your breakfast sandwich maker, it will be the fastest, easiest, and most enjoyable meal of the day, too!

Skipping breakfast is not just a disservice to your taste buds, it can be a problem for your whole body. People who don't eat the first meal of the day are found to be less productive at work, to have less mental clarity and energy throughout the day, and may find that they are deficient in important daily nutrients and minerals found in many fruits and vegetables. A little time and energy in the morning towards a healthy breakfast will keep you energized and focused during the mid-morning slump, save you money and your waistline on unnecessary snacking, and make you wish these delicious breakfast sandwiches weren't only for breakfast!

The Problems with Making a Quick and Healthy Breakfast

We all know what keeps us from starting the day with a delicious, healthy meal. There isn't any milk for the cereal, dried oatmeal is boring, and that single fried egg is beginning to look a bit sad. Better to grab a bag of chips at work or an energy drink at a convenience store on the way, right? Wrong! There's no better time than now to dust off your breakfast sandwich maker and start making quick and fun meals that you might have paid triple for in a restaurant, in the comforts of your own home!

Recipes with Minimal Steps and Easy Preparation

The recipes included in this book vary with preparation time, but should not take longer than a simple five minutes. The minimal steps include cleaning and preparing your breakfast sandwich maker, choosing and slicing any of your choice of delicious ingredients, such as fresh egg, cheeses, bacon, and fruit slices, and assembling the layers in the maker. Close the lid, set the timer, and get out a plate!

No Mess and Quick Clean-Up!

What about the arduous clean-up, you ask? Not a problem! Most breakfast sandwich makers have removable, dishwasher-safe parts that make cleaning up after a breeze. It'll make you wonder why you would ever scrub a greasy, egg-fried skillet again! A little wipe down of the cooking space, put away those fresh veggies and meats until tomorrow morning (if you can wait until then), and voila! A breakfast to make your cereal-eating coworkers' stomachs rumble with envy.

Fun, Healthy, and Easy-to-Make Recipes

These easy-to-make recipes will be a healthy, protein-filled start to your busy workday or a simple yet indulgent start to your restful Sunday mornings. Keeping a foundation of your favorite ingredients in the kitchen will make throwing together a tasty avocado, cheddar, and bacon English muffin sandwich or a succulent egg, maple sausage, and pancake sandwich easier than you ever imagined!

Variety of Recipes

With such a variety of fruit, veggie, meat, bread, and topping options, choosing a different recipe for each day makes your once dreaded morning routine a fun and exciting, not to mention delicious, experience! Whether you're gluten-friendly or gluten-free, vegetarian or hungry for meat, there are recipes and options for everyone to have the most hearty, simple, and scrumptious breakfast, lunch, dinner, and desserts! Take some time to stock up at your local grocer's on your favorite jams, cheeses, butters, fruits, bagels, muffins, and a carton of eggs, and get ready to make some delicious meals with breakfast sandwich maker!

Tips and Techniques

Cutting Down on Preparation Time

Vegetables

Once a week or so, after your weekly ingredients shopping, set aside some time to chop up your vegetables. Once sliced or diced, put the veggies into airtight containers or plastic bags and keep in the freezer, ready for easy access in the mornings. Don't forget to label with the date! Making sure your ingredients are fresh is important to making sure your breakfast is as healthy as possible.

Breads

Always keep a constant supply of fresh breads that fit into your sandwich maker. Try out some new kinds if you're used to the plain ole' bagels and white toasts.

- If you want to stick with bagels, try out blueberry, strawberry, maple flavored, or an old-fashioned everything bagel. They are also sold in a variety of mini flavors, if the size better fits your breakfast sandwich maker.
- English muffins can vary from wheat, multigrain, white, and even gluten-free!
- Biscuits can be made from sweet potatoes, buttermilk, and gluten-free flours like almond or sweet coconut. In this book, we will refer to the common Pillsbury biscuits that are sold in a tube of dough.
  - Pre-cook your biscuits according the packaging directions and freeze ahead of time to thaw for easy morning access.
- There's a variety of gluten-free sliced breads that come in flavors such as cinnamon raisin, wheat, and white. Like regular bread, simply cut a four inch circle out of two slices to fit comfortably into the breakfast sandwich maker.
- Small pancakes, about four inches, can be a fun and easy addition to your bread variety! Whether bought frozen and prepared or cooked ahead and frozen in an air-tight container until use, pancakes can be a great way to add a rich, maple flavor to any sandwich combination. Pancakes can easily be adapted to gluten-free diets as well.
- Frozen waffles are a cheap and simple alternative to bagels and muffins as well. Cut a bit around the waffle until it is about four inches across, and you have it! A delicious base for a sweet and slightly crunchy breakfast sandwich. Always keep waffles frozen until use, following all storage instructions according to the packaging.

Give them all a chance! You'll never know what amazing combination of flavors you could come across in trying out these breakfast sandwich recipes. Don't buy too many at once, however, unless you plan to store them in the freezer to keep them fresher for a little while longer.

Cheeses

Here's where the real fun comes in! There's a huge diversity in the world of these delicious dairies. There are always the classics, like cheddar, mozzarella, and parmesan, but take this chance to try out a few that you may have been afraid of before. Here's a list of a few of the most well-know:

Goat cheese:
- A soft earthy, tangy cheese made from goat's milk.
- Pairs well with vegetables such as bell peppers, onion, and garlic and with fruits such as apples, strawberries, and tomatoes.

Havarti:
- A semi-soft creamy, buttery cheese made from cow's milk.
- In stores you can find many different delicious types, such as dill and jalapeno, for an extra subtle bit of flavor.
- Havarti pairs well with bolder meats like ham and bacon, as well as sweeter fruits, such as strawberries and berry jams.

Mozzarella:
- A springy, stringy cheese originating in Italy, mozzarella has become one of the most recognizable cheeses.
- Primarily made from cow's milk, this cheese is semi-soft and milky and excellent at melty and browning beautifully over turkey, ham, and bacon.
- It pairs best with fruits and vegetables such as strawberries, pears, apples, peaches, onion, bell peppers, and most famously, tomatoes.

Brie:
- Another popular soft cheese, like goat, but with a nuttier, fruiter, and more mild flavor.
- Melty and buttery, it pairs well with heavier meats such as sausage, bacon, and smoked ham.
- Apples, pears, and berries taste even sweeter when together with brie, and spreads such as honey and berry jams bring out its delicious flavor as well.

Cheddar:
- A favorite of Wisconsians, cheddar cheese is sharp yet creamy cheese with a slightly hard, crumbly texture.
- It's the most widely bought and consumed cheese on earth, and for good reason: it pairs

well with so much! Particularly, apples, apricots, and pears, berry jams and compotes, and nuts.

- Experiment with sharp cheddar on a ham and pear English muffin sandwich, or a mild cheddar paired with a sweet blackberry compote.

Bleu:

- WIth its sharp and tangy flavor and association with mold, bleu cheese can be a hard sell. But don't be afraid! This cheese is perfectly safe and incredibly rich and tasty.
- It pairs best with sweet, crisp fruits such as pear and green apple and flavorful dried fruit like raisins, dates, and cranberries.
- With meat, bleu cheese is most exciting with ham, fish, and poultry.

Meats

There is an array of meats that can be mixed and matched with your breakfast sandwiches. Like cheeses, we all have our go-to favorites, but use this opportunity to try out some new kinds to pair well with your fruits, vegetables, and cheese to bring out a heartier flavor.

Pork:

Pork is a classic breakfast meat, but many other meat alternatives exist for those who are avoiding any extra calories. If you're more comfortable with what you know to be delicious, stock up on these savory varieties!

Always have a supply of bacon, a breakfast meat classic. Try out some different types such as the more thick cut Applewood bacon or a turkey bacon for lower calories. Pre-cook a batch and freeze or refrigerate for easy re-heating in the mornings. Try in the oven for the least amount of mess and greasy residue on your cooking space.

How to Cook Bacon in the Oven

1. Pre-heat the oven to 400 degrees.
2. Place one sheet of wax paper over a baking sheet. Lay strips of bacon across the baking sheet.
3. Place bacon in the oven and set your timer for seven minutes. After seven minutes, pull out the sheet and turn the wax paper. Put the bacon back into the oven and set your timer again for seven minutes.
4. Remove and let cool. Store in an air-tight plastic bag in the freezer or refrigerator.

Pre-cooked pork sausage patties are also a great staple for your meaty sandwiches, either with regular savory seasonings or a sweeter maple flavor.

Chorizo sausage in a tasty, spicy alternative to maple breakfast sausage. If unable to find pre-cooked, it is simple to pre-cook and freeze until use in the mornings.

How to Cook Chorizo Sausage in the Oven

1. Pre-heat the oven to 200 degrees.
2. Slice ½ inch thick slices of sausage off of the packaged sausage log.
3. Place a sheet of wax paper over a baking sheet. Arrange slices of Chorizo on the wax paper. Place sheet into the oven and set your timer for fifteen minutes.
4. Pull out the baking sheet and turn the wax paper. Place back into the oven and set your timer for another fifteen-twenty minutes, or until the meat reaches 165 degrees.
5. Remove and let cool. Store in an air-tight container in the freezer or refrigerator.

Sliced ham is always a favorite, and can be found pre-packaged at your local grocer. Many delis also fresh slice ham to your preferred weight, and can be a delicious, fresh alternative to regular lunch meat.

Poultry:

Whether classic sliced turkey breast or shaved chicken breast as an alternative to beef or pork, poultry is a delicious and healthy way to make an even more satisfying sandwich.

Turkey bacon is a great way to cut the fat of regular bacon, and contains important proteins that aid in digestion and B-12 (a necessary daily vitamin that supports the fatty substance that maintains and protects the nerves and nerve communication within the body).

Turkey sausage is another great alternative to pork, and can be bought in small patty sizes that will fit perfectly into your breakfast sandwich maker.

Classic turkey breast, like ham, can be found pre-packaged and sliced or at your local deli, ready to be sliced even fresher.

Breaded or grilled chicken breasts can be found frozen and prepackaged for a quick re-heat or cooked ahead and frozen.

Chicken adds a tasty extra juiciness to any breakfast sandwich.

Always make sure your chicken has an internal temperature of 165 degrees before consuming.

Sliced chicken breast, like turkey and ham, can be found in your local deli and sliced freshly to your preferred weight.

Vegetarian Options:

Many companies specialize in vegetarian sausage patty and bacon alternatives, such as Morningstar, a popular brand found in many grocery stores.

Most meat alternatives are made from vegetables and soy.

For many, these healthy, veggie-based varieties are indistinguishable from traditional meats and always pair well with fresh vegetables and delicious cheeses of your choosing.

Tofu can be bought at most grocery stores, and generally comes in a block kept moist in water.

Tofu can be fried and seasoned like regular meats, where it will lose its soft, silkier texture and become firm with a golden brown outer crust.

If you plan on trying it only occasionally, keep it in water in an airtight container in the freezer. Don't forget to drain before cooking!

Tempeh, like tofu, can be fried over a medium heat until firm and golden brown on the outside.

Pour over a little soy sauce or amino acids for an extra savory, salty, sausage flavor!

Keep frozen for up to three months, or defrosted in the fridge for up to six days.

Eggs

Some home breakfast sandwich makers have an option for cooking your eggs for you within the sandwich, but if yours doesn't have that option, or you're just concerned with the raw egg coming in contact with the bread, don't worry! Here's a trick that will keep your cook time as short as possible and leave with a variety of different eggs to try every day.

Quick and Delicious Eggs for a Week of Breakfast Sandwiches

1. First, find a muffin pan and spray with non-stick oil.
2. Crack a single egg into each muffin well. Sprinkle with salt and pepper.
3. Now here's the fun part! Top the uncooked eggs with crumbled bacon or thinly diced ham, chopped onion or bell pepper, or sprinkle with your favorite cheeses once you remove the eggs from the oven, while still hot.
   a. This way, every morning you have a new egg option for a delicious sandwich addition.
4. Bake for about fifteen minutes at 350 degrees. Pull out your eggs a bit earlier if you prefer a runnier yolk.
5. Store in an airtight container in the refrigerator for no longer than a week.
   a. To reheat, microwave for thirty seconds. If your sandwich maker has the option to cook and melt, put the cold egg straight into the maker, along with the cheese, bread, and toppings choices.

6. If you feel adventurous one day (or simply get tired of the same ole' single egg), try it scrambled!
    a. Whisk together six-eight eggs and ⅓ cup of milk and pour into the muffin wells.
    b. Sprinkle with salt and pepper, top with any savory additional ingredients, and cook for ten to fifteen minutes at 350 degrees.

Omelettes are a quick and easy alternative to fried or scrambled eggs, and a breeze to prepare in your breakfast sandwich maker!

1. First, whisk two or three eggs with two tablespoons of milk.
2. Pour half of egg mixture into both bread wells of your sandwich maker and sprinkle with salt and pepper if desired.
3. Top with any desired vegetables, cheeses, or meats, and pour over the remaining egg mixture.
4. Close the machine and cook for about two to three minutes, or until done.
5. Omelettes can also be prepared ahead of time and frozen in an airtight container until use.
    a. Make sure to thaw any individual omelettes for the next day in the refrigerator overnight or thaw under warm water before cooking into your sandwich.

Handy Guide to Food Storage and Safety

There is nothing more important to the integrity of your homemade sandwiches than making sure your ingredients are at their peak of freshness and accessibility. Keep this guide handy to make sure your fruits, vegetables, cheese, meats, and breads are of good quality, stored well, and are as ready as you are!

Fruits

For longevity and freshness throughout the week, it is important to make sure that the fruits are kept at their ideal temperatures.

Keep apples, apricots, and figs refrigerated; Keep avocados, bananas, peaches, pears, and tomatoes unrefrigerated.

Vegetables

Some vegetables can be tricky, but most will keep well in a refrigerator crisper for three to four days. It may be best to purchase veggies as needed, to avoid risk of waste.

Lettuce and other greens should be kept in an air-tight container with a damp cloth to avoid drying out, and for no longer than a week. Herbs as well, but the damp cloth isn't necessary.

Keep onions, garlic, and potatoes in a cool, dry, dark space.

Bread

Wrapped breads, such as sliced loaves, English muffins, and bagels, should be kept wrapped tightly in the original packaging.

At room temperature, bread should stay fresh for three to four days; If frozen, tightly wrapped bread can be kept for three months.

Bread that has begun to stale can be revived by being wrapped in a slightly damp cloth and microwaved for ten seconds or in the oven for five-ten minutes at 350 degrees.

Nuts

Nuts are a great protein-filled and crunchy addition to any breakfast sandwich.

They tend to go bad more quickly in warm, humid temperatures, but will stay fresh for up to a month at a cool room temperature, up to six months in the refrigerator, and for a year when kept frozen.

Keep a few handfuls of almonds, cashews, and walnuts for an oaky, nutty flavor to any combination.

Eggs

Making sure your eggs are stored well is incredibly important to the flavor and overall health safety of your breakfasts. Don't be nervous, however, while important, it's also pretty simple.

Keep uncooked eggs in the carton and inside the refrigerator instead of the door, to avoid other flavors and smells seeping into the thin delicate shell.

If you prefer the method of cooking multiple eggs at a time in a muffin pan, the cooked eggs kept frozen in an airtight container can be kept for up to a year!

Toppings

Sometimes, the most vital final touch of a delicious breakfast sandwich is the perfect saucy, jelly, or syrupy condiment topping.

Mayonnaise

This classic condiment and topping base can confusing as to whether it needs to be kept cold or at room temperature, but how it is stored does make a difference in longevity.

Unopened at room temperature, mayo can last up to a week past its labeled sell-by date.

Opened and kept refrigerated, mayo stays fresh for up to a month.

Jams and Pickles

The shelf life of fruity jams and jellies tends to depend on the ratio of fruit to sugar. The more sugary, the longer it can be kept. When it comes to pickled vegetables, such as classic dill pickles, peppers, sauerkraut, the shelf life is quite long.

Unopened at room temperature, jams will remain fresh about six months to a year past the sell-by date.

Jellies, which contain more sugar, can be stored unopened for one to two years.

Opened and kept refrigerated, both jams and jellies are fresh for up to a year past the date of being opened.

Pickled vegetables generally last for up to two years after the sell by date, whether kept refrigerated or in the pantry.

Cheese Spreads and Fruit Marmalades

For a creamy, rich addition to any bagel or English muffin breakfast sandwich, soft, spreadable dairy spreads like cream cheese are classic and delicious. For a flavorful fruity taste without all of the added sugar, preserves and marmalades are an excellent option. However, due to dairy and fresh fruit constraints, both toppings must not be consumed past the safe eat-by date.

All cheese spreads must be kept refrigerated. Unopened, they will remain fresh for about three to four weeks. Opened, they will only remain fresh for about one to two weeks.

Only cheese spreads unopened and wrapped in foil may be kept frozen for up to two months past the sell by date.

Fresh fruit preserves and marmalades remain safe to eat for about six to a year unrefrigerated, and nine months to a year refrigerated.

Butters, Nut Butters, and Other Toppings

There are so many options for any combination of ingredients and flavors to create the perfect final touch, but it's important to know how best to keep some of these more temperamental toppings.

Most apple, almond, and pumpkin butters, for example, tend to last for two to three months, whether kept opened and refrigerated or unopened at room temperature.

Butter and margarine should always be kept cold.

- If unopened, they remain fresh for three to four weeks refrigerated.
- Butter remains fresh for six to nine months kept frozen in foil or an airtight container.
- If the butter or margarine is opened, it may last for only up to two weeks refrigerated, but still for up to six to nine months frozen.

Maple syrup can last up to (or even longer than) eighteen months to two years in a plastic, unopened bottle.

- Once opened, keep refrigerated and the syrup may last four to six months.

Cottage cheese, a breakfast favorite for combining with fresh fruits, jams, and vegetables lasts for about a week to ten days refrigerated and up to three months frozen.

- Whether the packaging is opened or unopened, the shelf life is the same.

Tips for Safe Storage of Perishable, Semi-Perishable, & Non-Perishable Foods

All foods have a shelf life and safe temperature range to make sure that cold and warms foods remain at their safest for consumption.

Perishable Foods

Include fruits, vegetables, red meat, seafood, poultry, and dairy products. All cooked foods are perishable as well. Always keeps these foods at 40 degrees or below, refrigerated, or at 0 degrees, frozen.

- Hamburger and Other Ground Meats
  Refrigerated for only 1-2 days; Frozen for 1-2 months

- Fresh Red Meats
  Refrigerated for 3-5 days; Frozen for 6-12 months

- Fresh Poultry
  Refrigerated for 1-2 days; Frozen for 12 months

- Bacon & Sausage
  – Bacon
    Refrigerated for 7 days; Frozen for 1 month
  – Raw Sausage
    Refrigerated for 1-2 days; Frozen for 1-2 months

- Lunch Meats
  - Opened package or fresh deli sliced
    Refrigerated for 3-5 days; Frozen for 1-2 months
  - Unopened package
    Refrigerated for 2 weeks; Frozen for 1-2 months
- Salads (egg salad, chicken salad, tuna salad, pasta salad, etc.)
    Refrigerated for 3-5 days; Do not freeze
- Leftovers (Cooked meats or poultry)
    Refrigerated for 3-5 days; Frozen for 2-6 months

Semi-Perishable Foods

These are foods that remain fresh for about six months to a year if properly stored.

- Flour, grains, dried fruits, and dry mixes and seasonings.

Non-Perishable Foods

These are staple foods that generally will not spoil. However, if stored for a very long time, these foods may lose quality of peak flavor.

- Sugars, spices, dried beans and rice, and canned goods.

Temperatures and Timers

- Always keep a meat thermometer in your kitchen for making sure your foods have reached a safe internal temperature.
  - Ground beef should reach at least 160 degrees before consuming.
  - Whole and ground poultry should reach at least 165 degrees.
  - Raw beef steak, pork, and veal should reach at least 145 degrees.
- Keep a kitchen timer or stopwatch handy to always make sure your foods are perfectly cooked. Constantly pulled out of the kitchen to dress the kids or finish an email? Set the timer and you're all set! Many can be bought attached to a handy rope or chain so that you can carry it around your neck. You'll never overcook a delicious meal again!
- Always keep a kitchen scale nearby. This makes weighing out ounces of meats and cheeses easier than ever!

Use the Best Ingredients

Organic ingredients, which have become easier to find at grocery stores, as well as at your local farmers' market, are a great way to to make sure your fruits, vegetables, and nuts are the especially fresh and flavorful.

Match seasonal fruits and vegetables with the season for another opportunity to experience the freshest ingredients available in your sandwiches.

- Winter (December, January, February):
  Pears, clementines, dates, grapefruit, kale, kiwi, oranges, pomegranate, sweet potato, & tangerines.

- Spring (March, April, May):
  Apricots, artichokes, asparagus, green beans, limes, pineapple, spinach, & strawberries.

- Summer (June, July, August):
  Bell peppers, blackberries, blueberries, cherries, eggplant, figs, garlic, grapes, jalapeno peppers, peaches, plums, raspberries, tomatoes, & potatoes.

- Autumn (September, October, November):
  Brussel sprouts, cranberries, ginger, grapes, mushrooms, pineapple, pumpkin, & sunflower seeds.

Recipes

I. Traditional Breakfast Egg & Omelette Sandwiches

Classic Sausage, Egg, & Cheddar English Muffin Sandwich

Instructions:

1. Make sure that your breakfast sandwich maker is turned on and preheating.

2. Spread the butter over both sliced halves of the muffin.

3. LIft cover, top ring, and cooking plate. Place lower half of the muffin into the bottom bread well, cut side facing up. Top with sliced Cheddar.

4. Lower cooking plate and top ring. Spray surface and sides with oil to prevent sticking. Crack or place the egg into the hot well. (If you pre-cooked your eggs in a muffin pan, remove one egg from the freezer, thaw with warm water, and place in the egg well). Sprinkle with salt and pepper. Top with upper half of the muffin.

5. Lower cover and set your timer for five minutes.

6. Before opening, slide out the cooking plate to combine both halves of the sandwich.

7. Remove with a plastic spatula, serve, and enjoy!

Ingredients:

- 1-2 oz. pre-cooked sausage patty (heated to at least 40 degrees)
- 1 large egg
- 2-1 in. slices of Cheddar cheese
- 1 English muffin, halved (toasted or room temperature)
- 1 tbsp. softened butter
- Non-stick cooking spray
- Salt and pepper to taste

I. EGG & OMELETTE SANDWICHES

Classic Smoked Ham, Egg, & Havarti Bagel Sandwich

Ingredients:

2 slices of pre-cooked bacon, halved crosswise

¼ in. slice of pre-cooked smoked ham

1 large egg

2-1 in. slices of Havarti cheese

1 plain bagel, halved (toasted or room temperature)

2 tbsp. of butter

Non-stick cooking spray

Salt and pepper to taste

Instructions:

1. Make sure that your breakfast sandwich maker is turned on and preheating.

2. Spread each bagel half with butter. Place half of the bagel in the bottom bread well. Top with sliced Havarti and bacon.

3. Lower cooking plate and top ring. Spray surface and sides with oil. Crack or place one egg into the hot well. Sprinkle with salt and pepper if desired. Top with second half of the bagel.

4. Lower cover and set your timer for five minutes.

5. Before opening, slide out the cooking plate to combine both halves of the sandwich.

6. Remove with a plastic spatula, serve, and enjoy!

Classic Bacon, Scrambled Egg, & Cheddar Biscuit

Instructions:

1. Make sure your breakfast sandwich maker is on and preheating.
2. In a bowl, beat the egg and milk until smooth.
3. LIft cover, top ring, and cooking plate. Place one half of the biscuit in the bottom bread well. Top with sliced Cheddar and bacon.
4. Lower the top ring and cooking plate. Spray surface and sides with non-stick oil. Pour the whisked egg into the hot well. Sprinkle with salt and pepper if desired. Top with the second half of the biscuit.
5. Lower the cover and set your timer for five minutes.
6. Slide out the cooking plate to combine both sandwich halves.
7. Remove with a plastic spatula, serve, and enjoy!

Ingredients:

- 1 16 oz. Pillsbury biscuit, about ☒ of a roll (toasted or room temperature)
- 2 slices of pre-cooked bacon, halved crosswise
- 1 large egg
- 1 tsp. of milk
- 2-1 in. slices of Cheddar cheese
- Non-stick cooking spray
- Salt and pepper to taste

Classic Sausage, Mozzarella, & Cinnamon-Sugar Waffle Sandwich

Ingredients:

- 1-2 oz. pre-cooked sausage patty (heated to at least 40 degrees)
- 2-1 in. slices of Mozzarella cheese
- 1 large egg
- 2 tbsp. of butter
- 1 tsp of sugar
- ½ tsp. of cinnamon
- 2-4 in. pre-cooked frozen waffles (toasted or room temperature)
- Non-stick cooking spray
- Salt and pepper to taste

Instructions:

1. Make sure your breakfast sandwich maker is turned on and preheating.
2. In a bowl, combine butter, cinnamon, and sugar until well blended. Spread over one side of both waffles.
3. LIft cover, top ring, and cooking plate. Place one waffle into the bottom bread well, butter side up. Top with sliced cheese and the sausage patty.
4. Lower cooking plate and top ring. Spray surface and sides with non-stick oil. Crack or place egg into the hot well. Sprinkle with salt and pepper if desired. Top with the second waffle, butter side down.
5. Close the lid and set your timer for five minutes.
6. Slide out the cooking plate to combine both halves of the sandwich.
7. Remove with a plastic spatula, serve, and enjoy!

Classic Bacon, Tomato, and Pesto Cream Cheese Bagel Sandwich

Instructions:

1. Make sure your breakfast sandwich maker is on and preheating.
2. In a bowl, combine cream cheese and pesto and mix until blended. Spread the pesto cream cheese over each sliced half of the bagel.
3. Place one half of the bagel into the bottom bread well. Top with one slice of fresh tomato. Sprinkle with salt and pepper if desired. For added cheesiness, place the sliced Mozzarella over the tomato. Then top with the pre-cooked bacon.
4. Lower the cooking plate and top ring. Spray with non-stick oil. Crack or place egg into the hot well and sprinkle with salt and pepper, if desired. Top with the second half of the sliced bagel, cream cheese side down.
5. Close the cover and set your time for five minutes.
6. Before opening, slide out the cooking plate to combine both halves of the sandwich.
7. Remove, serve, and enjoy!

Ingredients:

- 2 slices of pre-cooked bacon, halved crosswise
- ¼ in. slice of fresh tomato
- 1 large egg
- 1 tbsp. of cream cheese
- ½ tsp. of basil pesto
- 1 bagel, halved (toasted or room temperature)
- Non-stick cooking spray
- Salt and pepper to taste
- 2-1 in. slices of Mozzarella cheese (optional)

Savory Sausage, Goat Cheese, & Garlic Cream Cheese English Muffin Sandwich

Ingredients:

1-2 oz. pre-cooked sausage patty (heated to at least 40 degrees)

1 tbsp. of Goat cheese

1 large egg

1 tbsp. of cream cheese

½ tsp. of minced garlic

Dash of paprika

Dash of rosemary

1 English muffin, halved (toasted or room temperature)

Non-stick cooking spray

Salt and pepper to taste

Instructions:

1. Make sure your breakfast sandwich maker is turned on and preheating.
2. In a bowl, combine the cream cheese, garlic, paprika, and rosemary and mix until well blended. Spread garlic cream cheese over each sliced side of the muffin.
3. Place lower half of the muffin into the bottom bread well. Top with crumbled goat cheese and the pre-cooked sausage patty.
4. Lower cooking plate and top ring. Spray the surface and sides with non-stick oil. Crack or place egg into hot well and sprinkle with salt and pepper if desired. Top with the upper half of the English muffin.
5. Close the cover and set your timer for five minutes.
6. Slide out the cooking plate in order to combine both halves of the sandwich.
7. Remove with a plastic spatula, serve, and enjoy!

Classic Bacon, Scrambled Egg, & Maple Butter Waffle Sandwich

Instructions:

1. Make sure your breakfast sandwich maker is turned on and preheating.
2. In a bowl, whisk butter until smooth. Slowly pour in maple syrup, continuing to whisk until well blended.
3. In a separate bowl, combine and beat the egg and milk until smooth.
4. Spread the maple syrup butter over a side of each waffle. Place one waffle in the bottom bread well, butter side up. Top with pre-cooked bacon.
5. Lower the cooking plate and top ring. Spray surface and sides non-stick oil and crack or place egg into the hot well. Sprinkle with salt and pepper if desired. Top with the second waffle, butter side down.
6. Close the cover and set your timer for five minutes.
7. Before opening, slide out the cooking plate to combine both halves of the sandwich.
8. Remove, serve, and enjoy!

Ingredients:

2 slices of pre-cooked bacon, halved crosswise

1 large egg

1 tsp. of milk

1 tbsp. of butter

¼ tbsp. of maple syrup

2-4 in. pre-cooked frozen waffles (toasted or room temperature)

Non-stick cooking spray

Salt and pepper to taste

Classic Smoked Ham, Scrambled Egg, & Swiss Biscuit Sandwich

Ingredients:

¼ in. slice of sliced smoked ham

1 large egg

1 tsp. of milk

2-¼ in. slices of Swiss cheese

1 16 oz. Pillsbury biscuit, halved (toasted or room temperature)

Non-stick cooking spray

Salt and pepper to taste

Instructions:

1. Make sure your breakfast sandwich maker is turned on and preheating.
2. In a bowl, beat together the egg and milk until smooth.
3. Lift cover, top ring, and cooking plate. Place the lower half of the biscuit into the bottom sandwich well. Top with sliced Swiss cheese and ham.
4. Lower cooking plate and top ring. Spray surface and sides with non-stick oil and pour the whisked egg into the hot well. Sprinkle with salt and pepper if desired. Top with the upper half of the biscuit.
5. Close the cover and set your timer for five minutes.
6. Before opening, slide out the cooking plate to combine both halves of the sandwich.
7. Remove with a plastic spatula, serve, and enjoy!

Sweet & Savory Sausage, Egg, and Apple Pancake Sandwich

Instructions:

1. Make sure your breakfast sandwich maker is on and preheating.
2. Place one pancake into the bottom bread well of the breakfast sandwich maker. Top with the slices of apple and pre-cooked sausage patty.
3. Lower cooking plate and top ring. Spray surface and sides with non-stick oil. Crack or place egg into the well and sprinkle with salt or pepper if desired. Top with the second pancake.
4. Cover and set your timer for five minutes.
5. Before opening, slide out the cooking plate to combine both halves of the sandwich.
6. If you're not running out the door, warm up the maple syrup in a small dish for dipping.
7. Remove with a plastic spatula, serve, and enjoy!

Ingredients:

- 1-2 oz. pre-cooked sausage patty (heated to at least 40 degrees)
- 1 large egg
- 2-¼ in. thick slices of red apple
- 2-4 in. pre-cooked pancakes (toasted or room temperature)
- ¼ cup of maple syrup (optional)

Caprese Bacon, Tomato, Mozzarella, & Fresh Basil English Muffin Sandwich

Ingredients:

2 slices of pre-cooked bacon, halved crosswise

¼ in. slice of fresh tomato

2-¼ in. slices of Mozzarella cheese

2 fresh basil leaves

1 English muffin, halved (toasted or room temperature)

Non-stick cooking spray

Salt and pepper to taste

Instructions:

1. Make sure that your breakfast sandwich maker is turned on and preheating.

2. Stack the basil leaves and roll into a tight tube. Cut the leaf into ribbons from right to left.

3. Lift the cover, tip ring, and cooking plate. In the bottom bread well, place the lower half of the English muffin. Top with the slices of Mozzarella cheese and bacon.

4. Lower the cooking plate and top ring. Spray surface and sides with non-stick oil. Crack or place egg into the hot well and sprinkle with salt and pepper if desired. Top with the basil ribbons and the upper half of the muffin.

5. Close the cover and set your timer for five minutes.

6. Before opening, slide out the cooking plate to combine both halves of the sandwich.

7. Remove, serve, and enjoy!

Hearty Bacon, Sausage, Crumbled Bleu Cheese, & Maple Aioli Bagel Sandwich

Instructions:

1. Make sure that your breakfast sandwich maker is on and preheating.
2. In a bowl, mix together mayo, maple syrup, and a small pinch of black pepper. Spread over both cut halves of the bagel.
3. Place one half of the bagel into the bottom bread well. Top with the sausage patty and crumbled Bleu cheese. Top with the pre-cooked bacon.
4. Lower cooking plate and top ring. Spray the surface and sides with non-stick oil. Crack or place egg into the hot well. Top with the upper bagel half, aioli side down.
5. Close cover and set your timer for five minutes.
6. Before opening, slide out the cooking plate to combine both halves of the sandwich.
7. Remove, serve, and enjoy!

Ingredients:

- 2 slices of pre-cooked bacon, halved crosswise
- 1-2 oz. pre-cooked sausage patty (heated to at least 40 degrees)
- 1 tbsp. of crumbled Bleu cheese
- 1 large egg
- 1 tbsp. of mayonnaise
- ½ tbsp of maple syrup
- 1 bagel, halved (toasted or room temperature)
- Non-stick cooking spray
- Salt and pepper to taste

Spicy Pepper Jack, Mozzarella, Avocado, & Fried Egg Biscuit Sandwich (Vegetarian)

Ingredients:

1-¼ in. slice of Mozzarella cheese

1-¼ in. slice of Pepperjack cheese

¼ Avocado, sliced

1 large egg

1 16-oz. pre-cooked Pillsbury biscuit, halved (toasted or room temperature)

Non-stick cooking spray

Salt and pepper to taste

Instructions:

1. Make sure your breakfast sandwich maker is turned on and preheating.

2. Finely dice both slices of cheese and blend together, making sure that both types of cheese are mixed throughout. (If you are using pre-shredded cheese, mix together about ⬚ of a cup each.)

3. Place one half of the biscuit into the bottom bread well and top with blended cheeses and sliced avocado.

4. Lower cooking plate and top ring. Spray the surface and sides with non-stick oil. Crack or place egg into the hot well and sprinkle with salt and pepper. Top with the other half of the biscuit.

5. Close cover and set your timer for five minutes.

6. Before opening, slide out the cooking plate.

7. Remove, serve, and enjoy!

Classic Sausage, Egg, & Cinnamon-Sugar Butter Pancake Sandwich

Instructions:

1. Make sure that your breakfast sandwich maker is turned on and preheating.
2. In a bowl, combine butter, sugar, and cinnamon until well blended. Spread over one side of each pancake.
3. Lift cover, top ring, and cooking plate. Place one pancake into the bottom bread well, butter side up. Top with American cheese and pre-cooked sausage patty.
4. Lower cooking plate and top ring. Spray the surface and sides with non-stick oil. Crack or place egg into the hot well. Sprinkle with salt and pepper to taste. Top with the second pancake, butter side down.
5. Close the cover and set your timer for five minutes.
6. Before opening, slide out the cooking plate to combine both halves of the sandwich.
7. If you have time, warm the syrup in a small dish for dipping.
8. Remove with a plastic spatula, serve, and enjoy!

Ingredients:

- 1-2 oz. pre-cooked sausage patty (heated to at least 40 degrees)
- 1 large egg
- 1 slice of American cheese
- 2 tbsp. of butter
- 1 tsp. of sugar
- ½ tsp. of cinnamon
- 2-4 in. pre-cooked pancakes (toasted or room temperature)
- ¼ cup of maple syrup (optional)
- Non-stick cooking spray
- Salt and pepper to taste

I. EGG & OMELETTE SANDWICHES

II. Famous Breakfast Sandwiches

Spicy Chorizo, Egg, & Goat Cheese on a French Baguette

Instructions:

1. Make sure that your breakfast sandwich maker is turned on and preheating.
2. Spread butter over both cut halves of the baguette. Place one half into the bottom bread well of the machine and top with crumbled Goat cheese and pre-cooked chorizo patty.
3. Lower cooking plate and top ring. Spray the surface and sides with non-stick oil. Crack or place egg into the hot well and sprinkle with salt and pepper. Top with the upper half of the baguette.
4. Close the lid and set your timer for five minutes.
5. Before opening, slide out the cooking plate to combine both halves of the sandwich.
6. Remove, serve, and enjoy!

Ingredients:

- 1-2 oz. pre-cooked chorizo sausage patty (heated to at least 40 degrees)
- 1 large egg
- 2 tbsp. of Goat cheese
- 1 tbsp. of butter
- ½ of a French baguette (or cut to fit bread well), halved (toasted or room temperature)
- Non-stick cooking spray
- Salt and pepper to taste

Bacon, Scrambled Egg, Tomato, & Herb Cream Cheese Bagel Sandwich

Ingredients:

2 slices of pre-cooked bacon, halved crosswise

1 large egg

1 tsp. of milk

¼ slice of fresh tomato

1 tbsp. of cream cheese

½ tsp of dried basil

Dash of dried parsley

Dash of dried rosemary

1 bagel, halved (toasted or room temperature)

Non-stick cooking spray

Salt and pepper to taste

Instructions:

1. Make sure that your breakfast sandwich maker is turned on and preheating.
2. In a bowl, combine and mix cream cheese, basil, parsley, and rosemary until blended and creamy. Spread over both halves of the bagel.
3. In another bowl, beat egg and milk until smooth.
4. Place one half of the bagel into the bottom bread well, cream cheese side up. Top with sliced tomato and bacon.
5. Lower cooking plate and top ring. Spray the surface and sides with non-stick oil. Crack or place egg into the hot well. Sprinkle with salt and pepper and top with the upper half of the bagel.
6. Close the lid and set your timer for five minutes.
7. Before opening, slide out the cooking plate to combine both halves of the sandwich.
8. Remove with a plastic spatula, serve, and enjoy!

Fried Bologna, White Cheddar, & Spicy Mustard on a French Baguette

A classic American breakfast, fried bologna is an easy and protein-filled breakfast meat option that both adults and kids with love!

Instructions:

1. Make sure that your breakfast sandwich maker is turned on and preheating.
2. In a pan, heat the oil until it begins to simmer. Place the bologna into the oil; Fry on each side until a crispy golden brown.
3. Spread the relish over the lower half of the baguette; On the upper half, spread the spicy brown mustard.
4. Lift cover, top ring, and cooking plate. Place the lower half of the baguette into the bottom bread well, relish side up. Top with sliced Cheddar and fried bologna.
5. Lower cooking plate and top ring. Spray the surface and sides with non-stick oil. Crack or place egg into the hot well. Sprinkle with salt and pepper and top with the second baguette half, mustard side down.
6. Close the lid and set your timer for five minutes.
7. Before opening, pull out the dividing disk so that both halves of the sandwich combine.
8. Remove, serve, and enjoy!

Ingredients:

- ¼ in. slice of bologna
- 1 tsp. of vegetable or olive oil
- 2-1 in. slices of white Cheddar
- 1 large egg
- 1 tbsp. of spicy brown mustard
- 1 tbsp. of sweet pickle relish
- ½ of a French baguette (or cut to fit bread well), halved (toasted or room temperature)
- Non-stick cooking spray
- Salt and pepper to taste

II. FAMOUS BREAKFAST SANDWICHES

Santa Fe Omelette & Cheddar English Muffin Sandwich (Vegetarian)

Ingredients:

1 large egg

1 tsp. of milk

1 tsp. of diced onion

1 tsp. of diced tomato

1 tsp. of green bell pepper

2-1 in. slices of Cheddar cheese

1 tbsp. of salsa (your preference)

1 English muffin, halved (toasted or room temperature)

Non-stick cooking spray

Salt and pepper to taste

Instructions:

1. Make sure your breakfast sandwich maker is turned on and preheating.
2. In a bowl, beat together the egg and milk until smooth.
3. Place one half of the muffin into the bottom bread well of the machine. Drizzle the muffin with the salsa and top with sliced Cheddar.
4. Lower cooking plate and top ring. Spray the surface and sides with non-stick oil. Pour half of the egg mixture into the well. Then sprinkle the pepper, onion, and diced tomato over the egg, and cover with the remainder of the mixture. Top with the upper half of the muffin.
5. Close the lid and set your timer for five minutes.
6. Before opening, slide out the cooking plate in order to combine both halves of the sandwich.
7. Remove with a plastic spatula, serve, and enjoy!

Glazed Maple & Brown Sugar Sausage with Brie Pancake Sandwich

A sweet, savory, and meaty special breakfast for any day of the week!

Instructions:

1. Make sure that your breakfast sandwich maker is turned on and preheating.
2. In a pan, heat the oil to a simmer. Rub both sides of the sausage patty with brown sugar and place into the pan, flipping both sides until cooked to a crispy brown.
3. Lift cover, top bread ring, and cooking plate. Place one pancake into the bottom bread well. Top with Brie slices and glazed sausage patty.
4. Lower top ring and cooking plate. Spray the plate and sides with non-stick oil. Crack or place egg into the well. Sprinkle with salt and pepper to taste. Top with the second pancake.
5. Close cover and set your timer for five minutes.
6. Before opening, slide out the cooking plate in order for both halves of the sandwich to combine.
7. Remove with plastic spatula. Pull sandwich apart, revealing the sausage. Drizzle with warm maple syrup. Put the sandwich back together and enjoy!

Ingredients:

- 1-2 oz. pre-cooked sausage patty (cooked to at least 40 degrees)
- 1 tsp. of warm maple syrup
- 1 tbsp. of brown sugar
- 1 tsp. of oil
- 2-1 in. slices of Brie cheese
- 2-4 in. pre-cooked pancakes (toasted or room temperature)
- 1 large egg
- Non-stick cooking spray
- Salt and pepper to taste

Bacon, Sharp Cheddar, and Fried Potato Biscuit Sandwich

Get ready to feel full! These lightly-fried potatoes will add an extra heartiness to this delicious breakfast sandwich.

Ingredients:

2 slices of pre-cooked bacon, halved crosswise

2-1 in. slices of sharp Cheddar cheese

1 large egg

2 slices of thinly sliced potato

1 tbsp. of oil, or as needed

1 tbsp. of ketchup

1 16-oz Pillsbury biscuit, halved (toasted or room temperature)

Non-stick cooking spray

Salt and pepper to taste

Instructions:

1. Make sure your breakfast sandwich maker is turned on and preheating.

2. In a pan, heat oil to a simmer. Place the potato slices into the oil to fry lightly, about one minute on either side.

3. Spread ketchup over the bottom half of the biscuit. Lift cover, top ring, and cooking plate. Place biscuit into the bottom bread well, ketchup side up. Top with sliced cheese, lightly fried potato slices, and bacon.

4. Lower cooking plate and top ring. Spray surface and sides with non-stick oil. Crack or place an egg into the well. Sprinkle with salt and pepper to your preference. Top egg with second biscuit half.

5. Close the cover and set your timer for five minutes.

6. Slide out cooking plate, lift cover and rings, and carefully remove sandwich.

New York Style "Everything" Bagel Sandwich

A classic favorite, this savory breakfast sandwich will make you feel like you're in the "City that Never Sleeps" (but loves to eat)!

Instructions:

1. Make sure your breakfast sandwich maker is turned on and preheating.
2. Spread butter over both halves of the bagel.
3. Lift cover, top ring, and cooking plate. Place one half of the bagel into the bottom bread well, butter side up. Top with cheese and bacon.
4. Lower the cooking plate and ring. Spray surface and sides with non-stick oil. Crack or place an egg into the well and drizzle with hot sauce.
5. Top egg with second half of the bagel, butter side down.
6. Close cover and set your timer for five minutes.
7. Slide out the cooking plate to combine both halves of the sandwich. Lift cover and ring.
8. Remove, serve, and enjoy!

Ingredients:

- 2 slices of pre-cooked bacon, halved crosswise
- 1 large egg
- 1 slice of American cheese
- 1 tsp. of hot sauce
- 1 "everything" bagel, halved
- 1 tbsp. of butter
- Non-stick cooking spray
- Salt and pepper to taste

III. Chicken and Turkey Sandwiches

Roasted Turkey Breast, Sharp Cheddar, & Cranberry Biscuit Sandwich

This breakfast sandwich is a great way to utilize your Thanksgiving leftovers (if there are any!)

Instructions:

1. Make sure your breakfast sandwich maker is turned on and preheating.
2. Spread cranberry chutney or jam on both biscuit halves.
3. Lift cover, top ring, and cooking plate. Place lower half of the biscuit into the bottom bread well, cranberry side up. Top with slices of Cheddar and sliced turkey breast.
4. Lower cooking plate and top ring. Spray surface and sides with non-stick oil and crack or place egg into the well. Sprinkle with salt and pepper if desired. Top the egg with the second half of the biscuit.
5. Close cover and set your timer for five minutes.
6. Slide out the cooking plate before opening, then lift cover and top ring.
7. Remove with a plastic spatula, serve, and enjoy!

Ingredients:

- 2 oz. of sliced roasted turkey breast
- 2 tbsp. of cranberry chutney or jam
- 2-1 in. slices of sharp Cheddar cheese
- 1 large egg
- 1 16-oz Pillsbury biscuit, halved (toasted or room temperature)
- Non-stick cooking spray
- Salt and pepper to taste

Roasted Turkey Breast, Spinach, & Sun-Dried Cream Cheese Bagel Sandwich

Ingredients:

2 oz. of sliced roasted turkey breast

2 tbsp. of cream cheese

1 ½ tsp. of chopped sun-dried tomatoes in oil

1 large egg

¼ cup of fresh baby spinach

1 bagel, halved (toasted or room temperature)

Non-stick cooking spray

Salt and pepper to taste

Instructions:

1. Make sure your breakfast sandwich maker is turned on and preheating.
2. In a bowl, combine cream cheese and sun-dried tomatoes until blended. Spread over both halves of the bagel.
3. Gather spinach into a stack and roll into a tight tube. Cut into thick ribbons from right to left.
4. Lift cover, top ring, and cooking plate. Place one half of the bagel into the bottom bread well, cream cheese side up. Top with sliced turkey breast.
5. Lower cooking plate and top ring; spray surface and sides with non-stick oil spray. Crack or place egg into the well. Sprinkle with salt and pepper if desired. Top with spinach ribbons and the upper half of the bagel.
6. Close lid and set your timer for five minutes.
7. Slide out the cooking plate before opening. Then lift cover and top ring.
8. Remove, serve, and enjoy!

Roasted Turkey Breast, Avocado Creme, & Provolone on a French Baguette

Once you learn how to make delicious avocado creme, you'll want to to add it to everything for a creamy, fresh flavor!

Instructions:

1. Make sure your breakfast sandwich maker is turned on and preheating.
2. In a bowl, blend together avocado and mayonnaise until whipped.
3. Gather the spinach into a stack and roll into a tight tube. Cut into thick ribbons from right to left.
4. Spread the avocado creme on both halves of the French baguette.
5. Lift the cover, top ring, and cooking plate. Place one half of the baguette into the bread well, creme side up. Top with Provolone.
6. Lower the cooking plate and top ring. Fill with sliced turkey breast and top with fresh spinach ribbons and the upper half of the French baguette.
7. Close cover and set your timer for five minutes.
8. Before opening, slide out the cooking plate. Then lift cover and top ring.
9. Remove, serve, and enjoy!

Ingredients:

¼ avocado, diced

⊠ cup of mayonnaise

2-¼ in. slices of Provolone cheese

2 oz. of sliced roasted turkey breast

¼ cup of fresh baby spinach

½ of a French baguette (or cut to fit sandwich well), halved (toasted or room temperature)

III. CHICKEN AND TURKEY SANDWICHES

Roasted Turkey Breast, Bacon, & Chipotle Aioli Biscuit Sandwich

Ingredients:

- 2 slices of pre-cooked bacon, halved crosswise
- 2 oz. of sliced roasted turkey breast
- 2-1 in. slices of Havarti cheese
- ⅓ cup of mayonnaise
- 1 chipotle pepper in adobo sauce, minced
- 1 tsp. of adobo sauce (from chipotle peppers)
- 1 tbsp. oil
- ¼ cup of fresh baby spinach
- 1 tbsp. of diced onion
- 1 tsp. of minced garlic
- 1 16 oz. Pillsbury biscuit, halved (toasted or room temperature)

Instructions:

1. Make sure your breakfast sandwich maker is turned on and preheating.
2. In a bowl, combine mayo, minced chipotle, and adobo sauce until blended.
3. Gather the spinach into a stack and roll into a tight tube; cut into ribbons from right to left.
4. In a pan, heat up oil and saute onion, garlic and spinach for two minutes. Drain excess oil after cooking.
5. Spread both biscuit halves with the chipotle aioli.
6. Place the lower half of the biscuit into the bottom bread well, aioli side up. Top with Havarti, bacon, and sauteed vegetables.
7. Lower cooking plate and top ring. Fill with turkey breast and top with the upper half of the biscuit.
8. Close the cover and set your timer for five minutes.
9. Before opening, slide out the cooking plate. Then lift cover and top ring.
10. Remove, serve, and enjoy!

Melty Mozzarella & BBQ Chicken on a French Baguette

This delicious sandwich is great for indoor barbeques and is sure to be a hit with adults and kids alike!

Instructions:

1. Make sure your breakfast sandwich maker is turned on and preheating.
2. In a bowl, mix together the turkey breast and BBQ sauce by hand until the sauce covers the turkey. Use more BBQ sauce if necessary.
3. In a pan, bring oil to a simmer. Add onions and saute for two-three minutes.
4. Spread mayonnaise over both sides of the halved baguette. Place one half into the bottom bread well of the machine. Top with cheese and sauteed onion.
5. Lower the cooking plate and top ring and fill with the BBQ chicken. Top with second half of the French baguette.
6. Close the cover and set your timer for five minutes.
7. Before opening, slide out the cooking plate. Then lift cover and top ring.
8. Remove with a plastic spatula, serve, and enjoy!

Ingredients:

- 2 oz. of sliced or shaved chicken breast
- 3 tbsp. of BBQ sauce
- 2-1 in. slices of Mozzarella cheese
- ¼ cup of minced onion
- 1 tbsp. of oil, or as needed
- ½ of a French baguette (or cut to fit bread well), halved (toasted or room temperature)
- 2 tbsp. of mayonnaise
- 1 tsp of balsamic vinaigrette dressing

Spicy Turkey Breast, Jalapeno, & Fresh Tomato Sourdough Melt

Ingredients:

2 oz. of sliced roasted turkey breast

2-1 in. slices of Pepper Jack cheese

1 pickled or fresh jalapeno, sliced

¼ in. sliced fresh tomato

2 tbsp. of mayonnaise

2 slices of Sourdough bread

Instructions:

1. Make sure your breakfast sandwich maker is turned on and preheating.
2. With a large cookie cutter, cut the Sourdough bread into four inch circles, or to fit the bread well of your machine.
3. Spread mayo on both slices of bread.
4. LIft the cover, top ring, and cooking plate; place one slice of bread into the bread well, mayo side up. Top with cheese, jalapeno slices, and tomato slice.
5. Lower cooking plate and top ring and fill with the sliced turkey. Top with second slice of Sourdough, mayo side down.
6. Cover and set your timer for five minutes.
7. Before opening, slide out the cooking plate. Then lift cover and top ring.
8. Remove with a plastic spatula, serve, and enjoy!

Buffalo Chicken and Bleu Cheese on Sourdough

Always a great spicy and creamy addition to any Super Bowl party! Serve with chips or fresh celery and carrot with a bleu cheese dipping sauce.

Instructions:

1. Make sure your breakfast sandwich maker is turned on and preheating.
2. In a bowl, mix together the buffalo sauce and chicken breast by hand until chicken is completely covered. Use extra buffalo sauce if necessary.
3. With a large cookie cutter, cut the bread into four inch circles, or to fit the bread well of your breakfast sandwich maker. Spread bleu cheese dressing over both slices.
4. Lift cover, top ring, and cooking plate. Place one slice of bread into the bread well, dressing side up. Top with tomato, cucumber, and bleu cheese crumbles.
5. Lower cooking plate and ring and fill with buffalo chicken. Top with the second slice of Sourdough, dressing side down.
6. Close the cover and set your timer for five minutes.
7. Before opening, slide out the cooking plate. Then lift cover and top ring.
8. Remove, serve, and enjoy!

Ingredients:

- 2 oz. of sliced or shaved chicken breast
- 2 tbsp. of buffalo sauce
- 2 tbsp. of crumbled bleu cheese
- 2 tbsp. of bleu cheese dressing
- 3 slices of cucumber
- ¼ in. slice of tomato
- 2 slices of Sourdough bread

Roasted Turkey Breast, Bacon, & Apple Club on CInnamon-Raisin Bread

Ingredients:

2 oz. of sliced roasted turkey breast

1 slice of pre-cooked bacon, halved crosswise

1 slice of fresh tomato

☒ cup of fresh baby spinach

2 thick slices of fresh apple

2 tbsp. of mayonnaise

2-1 in slices of white Cheddar cheese

Instructions:

1. Make sure your breakfast sandwich maker is turned on and preheating.

2. With a large cookie cutter, cut the bread into four inch circles, or to fit the bread well of your sandwich maker. Spread mayo over both slices.

3. Gather the spinach into a stack and roll into a tight tube. Cut into thick ribbons from right to left.

4. Place one slice of bread, mayo side up, into the bottom bread well. Top with cheese, tomato, apple, and bacon.

5. Lower the cooking plate and top ring and fill with the turkey breast. Top with fresh spinach and the second slice of cinnamon bread, mayo side down.

6. Cover and set your timer for five minutes.

7. Before opening, slide out the cooking plate. Then lift cover and top ring.

8. Remove with a plastic spatula, serve, and enjoy!

Chicken Breast, Apple Jelly, & Mozzarella Walnut Bread Sandwich

Instructions:

1. Make sure your breakfast sandwich maker is turned on and preheating.
2. With a large cookie cutter, cut the bread into four inch circles, or to fit the bread well. Spread apple jam or jelly onto one side of both slices of bread.
3. Gather the spinach into a stack and roll into a tight tube. Cut into thick ribbons from right to left.
4. Lift cover, top ring, and cooking plate. Place one slice of nut bread into the bottom bread well, fruit side up. Top with cheese and a slice of fresh apple for an additional juicy crispiness.
5. Lower cooking plate and top ring. Fill with sliced chicken breast and top with spinach and the second slice of bread, fruit side down.
6. Close the cover and set your timer for five minutes.
7. Before opening, slide out the cooking plate. Then lift cover and top ring.
8. Remove with a plastic spatula, serve, and enjoy!

Ingredients:

- 2 oz. of sliced or shaved chicken breast
- 2 tbsp. of apple jelly or jam
- 2-1 in. slices of Mozzarella cheese
- ¼ cup of fresh baby spinach
- 2 slices of walnut (or any nut) bread
- 1 thick slice of fresh apple (optional)

Chicken Breast, Fig Compote, & Brie English Muffin Sandwich

Ingredients:

2 oz. sliced or shaved chicken breast

2-1 in. slices of Brie cheese

2 tbsp. of fig compote

1 tbsp. of honey

1 English muffin, halved (toasted or room temperature)

Instructions:

1. Make sure your breakfast sandwich maker is turned on and preheating.
2. Spread honey on the lower half of the muffin and the fig compote on the upper half. Place the lower half into the bottom bread well. Top with brie.
3. Lower the cooking plate and top ring and fill with chicken breast. Top with upper half of the muffin, fruit side down.
4. Close the cover and set your timer for five minutes.
5. Before opening, slide out the cooking plate. Then lift cover and top ring.
6. Remove with a plastic spatula, serve, and enjoy!

Chicken Breast, Pepperoni, and Parmesan on a French Baguette

Have any pepperonis left from pizza night? Layer them up with a soft baguette and rich cheeses for a melty sandwich that kids and adults will love!

Instructions:

1. Make sure your breakfast sandwich maker is turned on and preheating.
2. Lift cover, top ring, and cooking plate. Place lower half of the baguette into the bottom bread well. Top with cheeses and one tablespoon of marinara sauce.
3. Lower cooking plate and top ring and fill with pepperoni. Cover with one tablespoon of marinara sauce and top with upper half of French baguette.
4. Cover and set your timer for five minutes.
5. Before opening, slide out the cooking plate. Then lift cover and top ring.
6. Remove, serve, and enjoy!

Ingredients:

- 2 oz. sliced or shaved chicken breast
- 2-1 in. slices of Mozzarella cheese
- 1 tbsp. grated or shaved Parmesan cheese
- 5-6 slices of pepperoni
- 2 tbsp. marinara sauce
- ½ of a French Baguette (or cut to fit bread well), halved (toasted or room temperature)

IV. Bacon and Pork Sandwiches

Smoked Ham, Brie, & Honey Biscuit Sandwich

Instructions:

1. Make sure your breakfast sandwich maker is turned on and preheating.
2. Spread the strawberry jelly on the lower half of the biscuit and the honey on the upper half. Place the bottom half into the bottom bread well and top with sliced Brie.
3. Lower the cooking plate and top ring and fill with sliced ham. Cover with upper half of the biscuit.
4. Close lid and set your timer for five minutes.
5. Before opening, slide out the cooking plate. Then lift cover and top ring.
6. Remove, serve, and enjoy!

Ingredients:

2 oz. sliced smoked ham

2-1 in. slices of Brie cheese

2 tbsp. of honey

1 tbsp. of strawberry jelly

1 16 oz. Pillsbury Biscuit, halved (toasted or room temperature)

Smoked Ham, Gouda, & Blackberry Jam Waffle Sandwich

Ingredients:

2 oz. of sliced smoked ham

2-1 in. slices of Gouda cheese

2 tbsp. of blackberry jam

1 tbsp. of butter

1 tsp. of sugar

Dash of cinnamon

2-4 in. pre-cooked frozen waffles (toasted or room temperature)

Instructions:

1. Make sure your breakfast sandwich maker is turned on and preheating.
2. In a bowl, combine butter, cinnamon, and sugar and mix until well blended. Spread over one side of one waffle. Spread blackberry jam on one side of the other waffle.
3. LIft the cover, top ring, and cooking plate. Place one waffle in the bottom bread well, fruit side up. Top with Gouda.
4. Lower the cooking plate and top ring. Fill with sliced smoked ham and top with the second waffle, butter side down.
5. Close the lid and set your timer for five minutes.
6. Before opening, slide out the cooking plate. Then lift cover and top ring.
7. Remove with a plastic spatula, serve, and enjoy!

Bacon, Fresh Peach, & Mozzarella Melt on Wheat

A sweet and savory sandwich that's perfect for breakfast, lunch, or even dinner! Perfect for warm summer nights. try fresh peaches from your local farmer's market for extra fresh juiciness.

Instructions:

1. Make sure your breakfast sandwich maker is turned on and preheating.
2. Use a large cookie cutter to cut the bread into four inch circles, or to fit the bread well. Spread a thin layer of peanut butter on both slices of bread.
3. Place one slice of wheat into the bottom bread well, peanut butter side up. Top with Mozzarella cheese and peach slices.
4. Lower the cooking plate and fill with bacon. Cover with second slice of wheat bread, peanut butter side down.
5. Lower the lid and set your timer for five minutes.
6. Before opening, slide out the cooking plate. Then lift cover and top ring.
7. Remove with a plastic spatula, serve, and enjoy!

Ingredients:

- 2 slices of pre-cooked bacon, halved crosswise
- 2-1 in. slices of Mozzarella cheese
- 2 slices of fresh peach
- 1 tbsp. of peanut butter
- 2 slices of wheat bread (toasted or room temperature)

Chorizo, Grilled Peppers, & Mozzarella English Muffin Sandwich

Ingredients:

- ¼ in. pre-cooked chorizo sausage patty (heated to at least 40 degrees)
- ¼ cup diced bell peppers
- 2 tbsp. of oil
- 2-1 in. slices of Mozzarella cheese
- 1 tbsp. of spicy brown mustard
- 1 English muffin, halved (toasted or room temperature)

Ingredients:

1. Make sure your breakfast sandwich maker is turned on and preheating.
2. In a pan, heat the oil until it begins to pop. Saute bell peppers for two-three minutes.
3. Spread mustard over the bottom half of the muffin.
4. Lift the cover, top ring, and cooking plate; Place the English muffin half with mustard on the bottom bread well. Top with cheese and sauteed peppers.
5. Lower the cooking plate and top ring; Fill with the chorizo patty (thawed or heated to at least 40 degrees). Top with Second half of English muffin.
6. Lower the cover and set your timer for five minutes.
7. Before opening, slide out the cooking plate. Then lift cover and top ring.
8. Remove with a plastic spatula, serve, and enjoy!

Pork Tenderloin, Apple, and White Cheddar on a French Baguette

Leftover pork chops or tenderloin have never tasted better with fresh sliced apple and melty Cheddar!

Instructions:

Make sure your breakfast sandwich maker is turned on and preheating.

In a bowl, combine dijon mustard and mayo until well blended. Spread over both halves of the baguette.

Place one half of the baguette into the bottom bread well. Top with cheddar and apple slices.

Lower the cooking plate and top ring; Fill with the slice of tenderloin. Top with arugula and the second half of the baguette.

Close the cover and set your timer for five minutes.

Before opening, slide out the cooking plate. Then lift cover and top ring.

Remove with a plastic spatula, serve, and enjoy!

Ingredients:

¼ in. sliced pork tenderloin

2 slices of fresh red apple

2-1 in. slices of mild white Cheddar cheese

¼ cup of arugula

1 tbsp. of dijon mustard

1 tbsp of mayonnaise

½ of a French baguette (or cut to fit bread well), halved (toasted or room temperature)

IV. BACON AND PORK SANDWICHES

Smoked Ham, Pear, & Brie on a Croissant

Ingredients:

2 oz. of sliced smoked ham

2 slices of fresh pear

¼ cup of arugula

2-1 in. slices of Brie cheese

2 tbsp. of strawberry jam or jelly

1 croissant, halved (toasted or room temperature)

Instructions:

1. Make sure your breakfast sandwich maker is turned on and preheating.
2. Spread jam or jelly onto both halves of the croissant.
3. Place one half of the croissant into the bottom bread well. Top with sliced Brie and pear.
4. Lower cooking plate and top ring; Fill with sliced smoked ham. Top with fresh arugula and second half of the croissant.
5. Close the cover and set your timer for five minutes.
6. Slide out the cooking plate and lift the cover and top ring.
7. Remove with a plastic spatula, serve, and enjoy!

Hawaiian Pork Tenderloin & Fresh Pineapple on a Soft Roll

No one else on board with Hawaiian style on pizza night? Make everyone envious of your fresh pineapple and savory pork sandwich.

Instructions

1. Make sure your breakfast sandwich maker is turned on and preheating.
2. Lift the cover, top ring, and cooking plate. Place one half of the soft roll into the bottom bread well. Top with Mozzarella, pineapple, and slice of tenderloin.
3. Lower cooking plate and top ring; Spray surface and sides with non-stick oil. Crack or place egg into the well. Sprinkle with salt and pepper. Top with second half of the soft roll.
4. Close lid and set your timer for five minutes.
5. Slide out the cooking plate and lift the cover and top ring.
6. Remove, serve, and enjoy!

Ingredients:

- ¼ in. slice of pork tenderloin
- 1 large egg
- 1 thick slice of fresh pineapple
- 2-1 in. slices of Mozzarella
- 1 soft roll, halved (toasted or room temperature)
- Non-stick cooking spray
- Salt and pepper to taste

V. Beef Sandwiches

Shaved Steak, White Cheddar, & Caramelized Onion Sourdough Melt

Instructions:

1. Make sure your breakfast sandwich maker is turned on and preheating.
2. With a large cookie cutter, cut the bread into four inch circles, or to fit the bottom bread well of the sandwich maker. Spread mayo over one side of both slices.
3. In a pan, bring butter and oil to a simmer. Then add sliced onion and cook until translucent.
4. Gather the spinach into a stack and roll into a tight tube. Cut into thick ribbons from right to left.
5. Place one slice of Sourdough into the bottom bread well. Top with Mozzarella and caramelized onion.
6. Lower cooking plate top ring; Fill with steak and top with fresh spinach ribbons. Cover with second slice of Sourdough, mayo side down.
7. Close cover and set your timer for five minutes.
8. Slide out the cooking plate and lift the cover and top ring.
9. Remove, serve, and enjoy!

Ingredients:

- 2 oz. of shaved or thinly sliced steak
- 2-1 in. slices of white Cheddar
- ¼ cup sliced onion
- 1 tbsp. of oil
- 1 tsp. of butter
- ¼ cup of fresh baby spinach
- 2 tbsp. of mayonnaise
- 2 slices of Sourdough bread (toasted or room temperature)

V. BEEF SANDWICHES

Meatball Marinara with Goat Cheese & Mozzarella on a French Baguette

Ingredients:

1 pre-cooked frozen meatball, sliced

2 tbsp. of marinara

1 tbsp. of Goat cheese

2-1 in. slices of Mozzarella cheese

¼ cup of fresh arugula

1 tbsp. of oil

½ of a French baguette (or cut to fit bottom bread well), halved (toasted or room temperature)

Instructions:

1. Make sure your breakfast sandwich maker is turned on and preheating.
2. Brush one side of both baguette halves with oil.
3. Lift cover, top ring, and cooking plate; Place one half of the baguette into the bottom bread well, oil side up. Top with sliced Mozzarella and crumbled Goat cheese.
4. Lower cooking plate and top ring: Fill with sliced meatball and marinara and top with second half of the French baguette, oil side down.
5. Lower cover and set your timer for five minutes.
6. Before opening, slide out the cooking plate. Then lift the cover and top ring.
7. Remove, serve, and enjoy!

V. BEEF SANDWICHES

Roast Beef, Provolone, & Horseradish Aioli on a Soft Roll

Instructions:

1. Make sure your breakfast sandwich maker is turned on and preheating.
2. In a bowl, mix together mayo and horseradish until blended. Spread over the upper half of the roll. Spread dijon mustard over the lower half of the roll.
3. Place one half of the roll in the bottom bread well, topping side up. Cover with sliced Provolone.
4. Lower cooking plate and top ring; Fill with roast beef and top with fresh arugula. Cover with second half of the soft roll, topping side down.
5. Before opening, slide out the cooking plate. Then lift the cover and top ring.
6. Remove, serve, and enjoy!

Ingredients:

- 2 oz. of sliced roast beef
- 2-1 in. slices of Provolone cheese
- 1 tbsp. of mayo
- 1 tsp. of horseradish
- 1 tbsp. of dijon mustard
- ¼ cup of fresh arugula
- 1 soft roll, halved (toasted or room temperature)

Shaved Steak, White Cheddar, & BBQ Aioli Bagel Sandwich

Ingredients:

2 oz. of shaved or sliced steak

2-1 in. slices of white Cheddar

1 tbsp. of BBQ sauce

2 tbsp. of mayonnaise

¼ cup of fresh spinach

1 bagel, halved (toasted or room temperature)

Instructions:

1. Make sure your breakfast sandwich maker is turned on and preheating.
2. In a bowl, mix together BBQ sauce and mayo until well blended. Spread over one side of each bagel half.
3. Gather spinach into a stack and roll into a tight tube. Cut into thick ribbons from right to left.
4. Lift cover, top ring, and cooking plate. Place the lower half of the bagel into the bottom bread well, aioli side up. Top with sliced white Cheddar.
5. Lower cooking plate and top ring; Fill with steak and top with fresh spinach ribbons. Top with the upper half of the bagel, aioli side down.
6. Close the lid and set your timer for five minutes.
7. Before opening, slide out the cooking plate. Then lift the cover and top ring.
8. Remove with a plastic spatula, serve, and enjoy!

VI. Calorie-Conscious

Roasted Turkey Breast, Asparagus, & Honey Goat Cheese on Wheat

VI. CALORIE-CONSCIOUS

Ingredients:

2 oz. of sliced roasted turkey breast

2 asparagus stalks, halved crosswise

2 tbsp. of oil

1 tbsp. of honey

2 tbsp. of Goat cheese

2-1 in. slices of Mozzarella cheese

2 slices of wheat bread (toasted or room temperature)

Salt and pepper to taste

Instructions:

1. Make sure your breakfast sandwich maker is turned on and preheating.

2. In a bowl, mix together by hand the asparagus, oil, and salt and pepper until asparagus is coated. Place into a hot pan and saute for three minutes, turning stalks evenly.

3. With a large cookie cutter, cut wheat slices into four inch circles, or to fit the bottom bread well of your machine.

4. In a bowl, combine and mix honey and Goat cheese until well blended. Spread over one side of one slice of bread.

5. Place the plain slice of bread into the bottom bread well. Top with Mozzarella slices and cooked asparagus stalks.

6. Lower cooking plate and top ring; Fill with turkey breast and top with second slice of wheat bread, Goat cheese side down.

7. Close cover and set your timer for five minutes.

8. Before opening, slide out the cooking plate. Then lift the cover and top ring.

9. Remove with a plastic spatula, serve, and enjoy!

Sharp Cheddar, Apple, & Spicy Horseradish Mustard on Wheat (Vegetarian)

Instructions:

1. Make sure your breakfast sandwich maker is turned on and preheating.
2. With a large cookie cutter, cut wheat bread slices into four inch circles, or to fit your breakfast sandwich maker.
3. In a bowl, blend together the mustard and horseradish. Spread over one side of both slices of bread. Place one slice of bread into the bottom bread well, mustard side up. Top with sliced Cheddar and apple.
4. Lower cooking plate and top ring. Fill with sliced turkey breast and top with fresh arugula. Cover with second slice of wheat bread, mustard side down.
5. Cover and set your timer for five minutes.
6. Before opening, slide out the cooking plate. Then lift the cover and top ring.
7. Remove with a plastic spatula, serve, and enjoy!

Ingredients:

- 2-1 in. slices of sharp Cheddar cheese
- 2 thick slices of fresh red apple
- 2 tsp. of horseradish
- 2 tbsp. of spicy brown mustard
- ¼ cup of arugula
- 2 slices of wheat bread (toasted or room temperature)

Peach, Mozzarella, & Basil Pesto Greek Yogurt English Muffin Sandwich (Vegetarian)

VI. CALORIE-CONSCIOUS

Ingredients:

2 thick slices of fresh peach

2-1 in. slices of mozzarella

2 tbsp. of greek yogurt

1 tsp. of basil pesto

½ cup of fresh spinach

1 English muffin, halved (toasted or room temperature)

Instructions:

1. Make sure your breakfast sandwich maker is turned on and preheating.
2. In a bowl, mix together Greek yogurt and pesto until well blended. Spread over both halves of the muffin.
3. Gather spinach into a stack and roll into a tight tube. Cut into thick ribbons from right to left.
4. Lift cover, top ring, and cooking plate. Place lower half of the muffin into the bottom bread well. Top with sliced Mozzarella.
5. Lower cooking plate and top ring; Fill with sliced peach and top with fresh spinach ribbons. Cover with second half of the English muffin.
6. Close the lid and set your timer for five minutes.
7. Before opening, slide out the cooking plate. Then lift the cover and top ring.
8. Remove with a plastic spatula, serve, and enjoy!

Mediterranean Feta, Spinach, & Sun-Dried Tomato on Pita (Vegetarian)

A crisp and fresh sandwich for any lunch or dinner that everyone will love! Substitute Greek yogurt for a creamy, filling base instead of cream cheeses.

Instructions:

1. Make sure your breakfast sandwich maker is turned on and preheating.
2. Gather spinach into a stack and roll into a tight tube. Cut into thick ribbons from right to left.
3. In a bowl, mix together balsamic dressing and Greek yogurt until well blended. Spread over one side of each piece of pita. Top with crumbled feta and sun-dried tomatoes.
4. Lower cooking plate and top ring. Fill with sliced cucumber and fresh spinach. Top with the second slice of pita.
5. Cover and set your timer for five minutes.
6. Before opening, slide out the cooking plate. Then lift the cover and top ring.
7. Remove with a plastic spatula, serve, and enjoy!

Ingredients:

- 2 tbsp. of crumbled Feta cheese
- ¼ cup of fresh spinach
- 2 tbsp. of chopped sun-dried tomatoes in oil
- 3 slices of fresh cucumber
- 2 tbsp. of balsamic vinaigrette dressing
- 1 tbsp. of Greek yogurt
- 2 slices of mini pitas, or cut to fit your breakfast sandwich maker (toasted or room temperature)

VI. CALORIE-CONSCIOUS

Turkey Bacon, Sauteed Veggies, and Goat Cheese on Pita

Ingredients:

2 slices of pre-cooked turkey bacon, halved crosswise

¼ cup sliced squash and zucchini

¼ slice of onion

1 tsp. of minced garlic

2 tbsp. of oil

2 tbsp. of Goat cheese

2-1 in. slices of Mozzarella cheese

2 slices of mini pitas, or cut to fit your breakfast sandwich maker (toasted or room temperature)

Instructions:

1. Make sure your breakfast sandwich maker is turned on and preheating.
2. In a pan, bring oil to a sizzle. Then add squash, zucchini, onion, and minced garlic (keep onion rings intact, but separated). Saute for three-five minutes.
3. Place one piece of pita into the bottom bread well. Top with sliced Mozzarella cheese and turkey bacon.
4. Lower the cooking plate and top ring. Fill with (drained) sauteed vegetables and top with crumbled goat cheese Cover with second piece of pita bread.
5. Close the lid and set your timer for five minutes.
6. Before opening, slide out the cooking plate. Then lift the cover and top ring.
7. Remove with a plastic spatula, serve, and enjoy!

Roasted Turkey Breast, Parmesan, and Basil Pesto Aioli on Wheat

Instructions:

1. Make sure your breakfast sandwich maker is turned on and preheating.
2. With a large cookie cutter, cut bread into four inch circles, or to fit your breakfast sandwich maker.
3. In a bowl, mix together basil pesto and light mayo. Spread a thin layer over one side of both slices of bread.
4. Place one slice into the bottom bread well, mayo side up. Top with sliced cheese.
5. Lower cooking plate and top ring. Fill with turkey breast and top with fresh arugula. Cover with second slice of wheat, mayo side down.
6. Cover and set your timer for five minutes.
7. Before opening, slide out the cooking plate. Then lift the cover and top ring.
8. Remove with a plastic spatula, serve, and enjoy!

Ingredients:

- 2 oz. of sliced roasted turkey breast
- 2-¼ in. slices of Parmesan cheese
- 2 tbsp. light mayonnaise
- 1 tsp. of basil pesto
- ¼ cup of fresh arugula
- 2 slices of wheat bread (toasted or room temperature)

VI. CALORIE-CONSCIOUS

Pan-Fried Tofu, Spinach, and Honey Ricotta on a French Baguette (Vegetarian)

Ingredients:

2-¼ inch slices of tofu

1 tsp. of garlic salt

1 tsp. of black pepper

2 tbsp. of oil

½ cup of fresh spinach

¼ in. slice of fresh tomato

2 tbsp. of Ricotta cheese

1 tbsp. of honey

½ of a French baguette (or cut to fit bottom bread well), halved (toasted or room temperature)

Instructions:

1. Make sure your breakfast sandwich maker is turned on and preheating.

2. In a pan, bring oil to a simmer. Season both sides of tofu slices with garlic salt and pepper. Fry lightly in oil until all sides are a golden brown, about five minutes.

3. Gather spinach into a stack and roll into a tight tube. Cut into thick ribbons from right to left.

4. In a bowl, mix together Ricotta and honey until well blended. Spread over both halves of the baguette. Place one half into the bottom bread well. Top with sliced tomato.

5. Lower the cooking plate and top ring. FIll with tofu and top with fresh spinach ribbons. Cover with top slice of the French baguette.

6. Close lid and set your timer for five minutes.

7. Before opening, slide out the cooking plate. Then lift the cover and top ring.

8. Remove, serve, and enjoy!

Sauteed Kale & Garlic with Havarti Melt on Wheat (Vegetarian)

Instructions:

1. Make sure your breakfast sandwich maker is turned on and preheating.
2. In a pan, bring oil to a simmer. Add kale, garlic, and onion and saute for three-five minutes.
3. With a large cookie cutter, cut bread into four inch. circles, or to fit your breakfast sandwich maker.
4. Lift cover, top ring, and cooking plate. Place one slice of bread into the bottom bread well. Top with sliced Havarti and tomato.
5. Lower cooking plate and top ring; FIll with sauteed kale and veggies. Top with second slice of wheat bread.
6. Cover and set your timer for five minutes.
7. Before opening, slide out the cooking plate. Then lift the cover and top ring.
8. Remove with a plastic spatula, serve, and enjoy!

Ingredients:

- ½ cup of fresh kale
- 1 tbsp. of minced garlic
- ¼ in. sliced onion
- 2 tbsp. of oil
- 2-¼ in. sliced Havarti cheese
- ¼ slice of fresh tomato
- 2 slices of wheat bread (toasted or room temperature)

Turkey Bacon, Avocado, & White Cheddar Wheat Melt

Ingredients:

- 2 slices of pre-cooked turkey bacon, halved crosswise
- ¼ avocado, sliced
- 2-¼ in. slices of white Cheddar cheese
- ¼ cup of fresh spinach
- 2 slices of wheat bread (toasted or room temperature)

Instructions:

1. Make sure your breakfast sandwich maker is turned on and preheating.
2. Gather spinach into a stack and roll into a tight tube. Cut into thick ribbons from right to left.
3. With a large cookie cutter, cut bread into 4 in. circles, or to fit your breakfast sandwich maker.
4. Place one slice of bread into the bottom well and top with sliced Cheddar and bacon.
5. Lower cooking plate and top ring; Fill with sliced avocado and top with fresh spinach ribbons. Cover with second slice of wheat bread.
6. Cover and set your timer for five minutes.
7. Before opening, slide out the cooking plate. Then lift the cover and top ring.
8. Remove, serve, and enjoy!

Roasted Turkey Breast, Artichoke, & Sun-Dried Tomato Greek Yogurt on Pita

Instructions:

1. Make sure your breakfast sandwich maker is turned on and preheating.
2. In a bowl, mix together Greek yogurt and sun-dried tomatoes until well blended. Spread over one side of each piece of pita.
3. Lift cover, tip ring, and cooking plate; Place one piece of pita into the bottom bread well, yogurt side up. Top with sliced Provolone cheese and artichoke hearts.
4. Lower cooking plate and top ring. Fill with sliced turkey breast and top with arugula. Cover with second piece of pita, yogurt side down.
5. Cover and set your timer for five minutes.
6. Before opening, slide out the cooking plate. Then lift the cover and top ring.
7. Remove, serve, and enjoy!

Ingredients:

- 2 oz. of sliced roasted turkey breast
- 3 artichoke hearts, sliced
- ¼ cup of arugula
- 2 tbsp. of Greek yogurt
- 1 tbsp. of diced sun-dried tomatoes in oil
- 2-¼ in. slices of Provolone cheese
- 2 pieces of mini pita, or cut to fit your breakfast sandwich maker (toasted or room temperature)

VI. CALORIE-CONSCIOUS

Veggie Sausage, Soy Cheese, and Cherry Preserves English Muffin Sandwich (Vegan)

Ingredients:

1 pre-cooked frozen veggie sausage patty

2 oz. of shredded soy cheese

¼ cup of arugula

2 tbsp. of cherry preserves

1 English muffin, halved (toasted or room temperature)

Instructions:

1. Make sure your breakfast sandwich maker is turned on and preheating.

2. Spread fruit preserves over one side of both halves of the muffin. Place one half of the English muffin in the bottom bread well. Top with soy cheese.

3. Lower cooking plate and top ring; Fill with thawed or warmed veggie patty and top with arugula. Cove with second half of the muffin, fruit side down.

4. Close the cover and set your timer for five minutes.

5. Before opening, slide out the cooking plate. Then lift the cover and top ring.

6. Remove, serve, and enjoy!

Veggie Bacon, Pan-Fried Tofu, & Soy Cheese Melt on Wheat (Vegan)

Instructions:

Make sure your breakfast sandwich maker is turned on and preheating.

In a pan, bring oil and soy sauce to a simmer. Season all sides of the tofu with garlic salt and pepper. Place into pan and lightly fry on all sides for three-five minutes.

With a large cookie cutter, cut bread into 4 in. circles, or to fit your breakfast sandwich maker.

Lift cover, top ring, and cooking plate; Place one slice of wheat bread into the bottom bread well. Top with soy cheese and bacon.

Lower cooking plate and top ring. Fill with fried tofu and top with top with sliced tomato. Cover with second slice of wheat bread.

Close the cover and set your timer for five minutes.

Before opening, slide out the cooking plate. Then lift the cover and top ring.

Remove with a plastic spatula, serve, and enjoy!

Instructions:

- 2 pre-cooked slices of veggie bacon, halved crosswise
- 2-¼ in. slices of tofu
- 2 tbsp. of oil
- 1 tsp. of soy sauce
- 1 tsp. of garlic salt
- 1 tsp. of black pepper
- 2 oz. of shredded soy cheese
- ¼ in. slice of fresh tomato
- 2 slices of wheat bread (toasted or room temperature)

VI. CALORIE-CONSCIOUS

VII. Gluten-Free

Spicy Egg Salad, Bacon, and Tomato on Gluten-Free Bread

Without the extra spiciness, this classic chicken salad can be great for kids too!

Instructions:

1. Make sure your breakfast sandwich maker is turned on and preheating.
2. In a bowl, combine egg, mayo, and Sriracha sauce. Mix until well blended.
3. With a large cookie cutter, cut gluten-free bread into four inch circles, or to fit the bottom bread well of your breakfast sandwich maker. Spread Dijon mustard on one side of one slice of bread.
4. Lift cover, top ring, and cooking plate; Place the plain slice of bread into the bottom bread well. Top with spicy egg salad and bacon.
5. Lower cooking plate and top ring; fill with the slice of fresh tomato and top with second slice of gluten-free bread, mustard side down.
6. Cover and set your timer for five minutes.
7. Before opening, slide out the cooking plate. Then lift the cover and top ring.
8. Remove, serve, and enjoy!

Ingredients:

- 1 hard-boiled egg, minced
- 1 tsp of Sriracha sauce
- 1-2 tbsp. of mayonnaise
- 2 slices of pre-cooked bacon, halved crosswise
- 1 slice of fresh tomato
- 1 tbsp. of Dijon mustard
- 2 slices of gluten-free bread of your choice (toasted or room temperature)

VII. GLUTEN-FREE

Smoked Ham, Swiss Cheese, & Raspberry Preserve Gluten-Free English Muffin Sandwich

VII. GLUTEN-FREE

Ingredients:

2 oz. of sliced smoked ham

2-¼ in. slices of Swiss cheese

2 tbsp. of raspberry preserves

¼ cup of fresh spinach

1 gluten-free English muffin (toasted or room temperature)

Instructions:

1. Make sure your breakfast sandwich maker is turned on and preheating.
2. Gather fresh spinach into a stack and roll into a tight tube. Cut into thick ribbons from right to left.
3. Spread raspberry preserves on one side of both halves of the muffin. Place one half into the bottom bread well of your breakfast sandwich maker. Top with sliced Swiss cheese.
4. Lower cooking plate and top ring; FIll with sliced smoked ham and top with fresh spinach ribbons. Cover with second half of the English muffin, fruit side down.
5. Close the lid and set your timer for five minutes.
6. Before opening, slide out the cooking plate. Then lift the cover and top ring.
7. Remove, serve, and enjoy!

Dill Cream Cheese, Avocado, & Tomato Gluten-Free Bagel Sandwich (Vegetarian)

Instructions:

1. Make sure your breakfast sandwich maker is turned on and preheating.
2. In a bowl, combine cream cheese and fresh dill. Mix until well blended. Spread over both halves of your toasted or room-temperature gluten-free bagel.
3. Lift cover, top ring, and cooking plate; Place one half of the bagel into the bottom bread well. Top with avocado.
4. Lower cooking plate and top ring; Fill with tomato and top with second half of the bagel, cream cheese side down.
5. Cover and set your timer for five minutes.
6. Before opening, slide out the cooking plate. Then lift the cover and top ring.
7. Remove, serve, and enjoy!

Ingredients:

2 tbsp. of cream cheese

1 tsp. of fresh dill, minced

¼ of avocado, sliced

¼ in. sliced fresh tomato

1 gluten-free bagel of your choice, halved (toasted or room temperature)

Huevos Rancheros Gluten-Free English Muffin Sandwich (Vegetarian)

Ingredients:

¼ of an avocado

1-2 tbsp. of mayo

2-¼ in. slices of Cheddar

1 large egg

1 tsp. of milk

1 tbsp. of salsa

1 gluten-free English muffin (toasted or room temperature)

Non-stick oil spray

Salt and pepper to taste

Instructions:

1. Make sure your breakfast sandwich maker is turned on and preheating.
2. In a bowl, beat together egg and milk until smooth. Set aside.
3. In another bowl, whisk together mayo and avocado until well blended. Spread over one side of both halves of the muffin. Place one half of the muffin into the bottom bread well. Top with sliced cheddar.
4. Lower cooking plate and top ring. Spray surface and sides with non-stick oil and crack or place egg into the hot well. Sprinkle with salt and pepper and top with salsa.
5. Cover and set your timer for five minutes.
6. Before opening, slide out the cooking plate. Then lift the cover and top ring.
7. Remove with a plastic spatula, serve, and enjoy!

Honey, Goat Cheese, & Fig Compote on Gluten-Free Cinnamon-Raisin Bread (Vegetarian)

Instructions:

1. Make sure your breakfast sandwich maker is turned on and preheating.
2. Use a large cookie cutter to cut slices of bread into four inch circles, or to fit your bottom bread well. Spread fig compote on one side of one slice and honey on one side of the other slice.
3. LIft cover, top ring, and cooking plate. Place one slice of bread into the bottom bread well, fruit side up. Top with crumbled goat cheese.
4. Lower cooking plate and top ring. Fill with fresh arugula and top with second slice of gluten-free bread, honey side down.
5. Close the cover and set your timer for five minutes.
6. Before opening, slide out the cooking plate. Then lift the cover and top ring.
7. Remove, serve, and enjoy!

Ingredients:

1 tbsp. of honey

2 tbsp. of Goat cheese

2 tbsp. of fig compote

¼ cup of arugula

2 slices of gluten-free cinnamon-raisin bread (toasted or room temperature)

Bacon, Bleu Cheese, & Sauteed Baby Bella Mushrooms on Gluten-Free English Muffin

VII. GLUTEN-FREE

Ingredients:

2 slices of pre-cooked bacon, halved crosswise

2 tbsp of crumbled Bleu cheese

¼ cup of fresh baby bella mushrooms

1 tbsp. of oil

1 tsp. of butter

2 tbsp. of mayonnaise

1 tbsp. of Dijon mustard

1 gluten-free English muffin (toasted or room temperature)

Instructions:

1. Make sure your breakfast sandwich maker is turned on and preheating

2. In a pan, heat oil and butter to a simmer. Add mushrooms and saute for 3-5 minutes.

3. In a bowl, combine mayo and Dijon mustard until well blended. Spread Dijonnaise over both halves of the muffin.

4. LIft cover, top ring, and cooking plate. Place one half of the gluten-free muffin into the bottom bread well. Top with crumbled Bleu cheese and bacon.

5. Lower cooking plate and top ring. Fill with mushrooms and top with second half of the muffin, Dijonnaise side down.

6. Cover and set your timer for five minutes.

7. Before opening, slide out the cooking plate. Then lift the cover and top ring.

8. Remove, serve, and enjoy!

Sauteed Pepper, Havarti, and Scrambled Egg Gluten-Free Wheat Sandwich (Vegetarian)

Instructions:

1. Make sure your breakfast sandwich maker is turned on and preheating.
2. In a pan, bring oil to a simmer. Add sliced onion, diced pepper, and kale. Saute for 3-5 minutes.
3. In a bowl, beat egg and milk until smooth. Set aside.
4. Place one slice of bread into the bottom bread well of your breakfast sandwich maker. Top with sliced Havarti.
5. Lower cooking plate and top ring. Spray with non-stick oil on surface and sides. Crack or place egg into the hot well. Sprinkle with salt and pepper. Top with (drained) sauteed vegetables.
6. Cover and set your timer for five minutes.
7. Before opening, slide out the cooking plate. Then lift the cover and top ring.
8. Remove, serve, and enjoy!

Ingredients:

¼ cup diced bell pepper
¼ in. slice of onion
¼ cup chopped kale
2 tbsp. of oil (or as needed)
2-¼ in. slices of Havarti cheese
1 large egg
1 tsp. of milk
2 slices of gluten-free what bread (toasted or room temperature)
Non-stick oil spray
Salt and pepper to taste

VII. GLUTEN-FREE

VIII. International Sandwiches

Spicy Mac n' Cheese, Jalapeno, & Bacon Melt on Sourdough

Savory, cheesy, spicy, meaty, and simple! This sandwich is a fun combination of favorite American flavors and ingredients.

Instructions:

1. Make sure your breakfast sandwich maker is turned on and preheating.
2. Prepare Kraft Easy Mac according to manufacturer's instructions.
3. Using a large cookie cutter, cut bread into 4 in. circles, or to fit bottom bread well.
4. In a bowl, combine chipotle powder and mayo. Spread aioli over one side of both pieces of bread. Place one slice of bread into the bottom bread well. Top with sliced cheese and bacon.
5. Lower the cooking plate and top ring. Spray surface and sides with non-stick oil. Fill with Easy Mac and top with sliced jalapeno. COver with second slice of Sourdough, mayo side down.
6. Cover and set your timer for five minutes.
7. Before opening, slide out the cooking plate. Then lift the cover and top ring.
8. Remove, serve, and enjoy!

Ingredients:

- ½ serving of Kraft Easy Mac
- 1 fresh or pickled jalapeno, sliced
- 2 tbsp. mayo
- ½ tsp. of chipotle powder
- 2 strips of pre-cooked bacon, halved crosswise
- 2-¼ in. slices of Pepper Jack cheese
- Non-stick oil spray
- 2 slices of Sourdough bread (toasted or room temperature)

VIII. INTERNATIONAL SANDWICHES

Italian Mozzarella Melt on a French Baguette

VIII. INTERNATIONAL SANDWICHES

Ingredients:

2 tbsp. of mayo

½ tsp. of garlic powder

½ tsp. of dried basil

1 tsp. of oil and vinegar

2 deli slices of pepperoni

2 deli slices of salami

2-¼ in. slices of Mozzarella cheese

½ of a French baguette (or cut to fit your bread well), halved (thawed or room temperature

Instructions:

1. Make sure your breakfast sandwich maker is turned on and preheating.

2. In a bowl, combine mayo and seasonings. Spread over one side of the lower half of the baguette. Brush oil and vinegar over the upper half of the baguette.

3. Place lower half of the bread into the bottom brad well. Top with sliced cheese.

4. Lower cooking plate and top ring. Fill with sliced meats and top with the upper half of the French baguette.

5. Cover and set your timer for five minutes.

6. Before opening, slide out the cooking plate. Then lift the cover and top ring.

7. Remove, serve, and enjoy!

Italian Florentine English Muffin Breakfast Sandwich (Vegetarian)

Instructions:

1. Make sure your breakfast sandwich maker is turned on and preheating.
2. In a bowl, combine Dijon mustard and Greek yogurt. Spread over one side of both halves of the muffin.
3. Gather spinach into stack and roll into tight tube. Cut into thick ribbons from right to left.
4. Lift cover, top ring, and cooking plate. Place one half of the bread into the bottom bread well. Top with sliced cheese.
5. Lower cooking plate and top ring. Spray with non-stick oil and crack or place into hot well. Sprinkle with salt and pepper. Top with fresh spinach ribbons and upper half of the English muffin.
6. Cover and set your timer for five minutes.
7. Before opening, slide out the cooking plate. Then lift the cover and top ring.
8. Remove, serve, and enjoy!

Ingredients:

2 tbsp. of Greek yogurt

1 tsp. of Dijon mustard

¼ cup of baby spinach

2-¼ in. slices of Parmesan cheese

1 large egg

1 English muffin, halved (toasted or room temperature)

Non-stick oil spray

Salt and pepper to taste

Parisian Smoked Ham, Pear, & Havarti on a French Baguette

A famous Parisian street sandwich with an added melty twist.

Ingredients:

2 oz. sliced smoked ham

2 thick slices of fresh pear

2-¼ in. slices of Havarti cheese

2 tbsp. of mayonnaise

1 tsp. of Dijon mustard

3 slices of dill pickle

¼ cup of fresh arugula

½ of a French baguette (or cut to fit bread well), halved (toasted or room temperature)

Instructions:

1. Make sure your breakfast sandwich maker is turned on and preheating.

2. In a bowl, combine mayo and Dijon mustard until well blended. Spread over one side of both halves of baguette. Place one half of the baguette into the bottom bread well. Top with sliced Havarti, fresh pear, and pickles.

3. Lower cooking plate and top ring. Fill with sliced ham and top with fresh arugula. Cover with upper half of the French baguette.

4. Cover and set your timer for five minutes.

5. Before opening, slide out the cooking plate. Then lift the cover and top ring.

6. Remove, serve, and enjoy!

VIII. INTERNATIONAL SANDWICHES

Cuban Medianoche on a Kaiser Roll

'Medianoche", meaning 'midnight', this traditional Cuban sandwich is a late-night favorite.

Instructions:

1. Make sure your breakfast sandwich maker is turned on and preheating.
2. In a bowl, combine mayo and mustard. Spread over both halves of the roll.
3. Lift cover, top ring, and cooking plate. Place the lower half of roll into the bottom bread well. Top with sliced Swiss cheese and pickles.
4. Lower cooking plate and top ring. Fill with sliced ham and drizzle with melted butter. Top with upper half of the roll.
5. Cover and set your timer for five minutes.
6. Before opening, slide out the cooking plate. Then lift the cover and top ring.
7. Remove, serve, and enjoy!

Ingredients:

- 2 tbsp. of mayonnaise
- 1 tbsp. of spicy brown mustard
- 2 oz. of sliced smoked ham
- 2-¼ in. slices of Swiss cheese
- 1 tbsp. of melted butter
- 3-4 sliced dill pickles
- 1 Kaiser roll, halved (toasted or room temperature)

VIII. INTERNATIONAL SANDWICHES

Chilean Chacarero on a Kaiser Roll

This classic Chilean street sandwich is easy, meaty, and full of tasty vegetables!

Ingredients:

2 oz. of sliced or shaved steak

¼ cup of boiled or steamed green beans (or cooked according to packaging)

¼ in. slice of fresh tomato

1 tsp oil and vinegar

1 pickled or fresh jalapeno, sliced

1 Kaiser roll, sliced

Instructions:

1. Make sure your breakfast sandwich maker is turned on and preheating.
2. Lift cover, top ring, and cooking plate. Place lower half of roll into the bottom bread well. Top with fresh tomato, oil and vinegar, and green beans.
3. Lower cooking plate and top ring. Fill with steak and top with sliced jalapeno and the upper half of the roll.
4. Cover and set your timer for five minutes.
5. Before opening, slide out the cooking plate. Then lift the cover and top ring.
6. Remove, serve, and enjoy!

English Chip Butty English Muffin Sandwich

This filling English favorite is fun and easy and loved by everyone! (You've probably been making it for years and never knew!)

Instructions:

1. Make sure your breakfast sandwich maker is turned on and preheating.
2. Drizzle melted butter over the inner side of both halves of the muffin. Spread H.P. or A.1. sauce over the lower half of the English muffin.
3. Place the lower half of the muffin into the bottom bread well. Top with sliced cheese.
4. Lower cooking plate and top ring. Fill with french fries and top with your choice of condiments. Cover with upper half of the English muffin.
5. Cover and set your timer for five minutes.
6. Before opening, slide out the cooking plate. Then lift the cover and top ring.
7. Remove with a plastic spatula, serve, and enjoy!

Ingredients:

- ¼ cup of pre-cooked french fries (warmed or room temperature)
- 2 tbsp. of melted butter
- 2-¼ in. slices of Mozzarella cheese
- 1 tbsp. of H.P. sauce or A.1. sauce
- 1 tsp of ketchup and/or mustard (optional)
- 1 English muffin, halved

Canadian Roast Beef and Mustard on Rye

Ingredients:

1 tbsp. of Montreal spice mix

2 oz. of sliced or shaved roast beef

2 tbsp. of spicy brown mustard

¼ cup of roasted red peppers, cut into strips

2-¼ in. slices of Provolone cheese

2 slices of Rye bread (toasted or room temperature)

Instructions:

1. Make sure your breakfast sandwich maker is turned on and preheating.
2. Rub Montreal spice mix over sliced or shaved roast beef.
3. With a large cookie cutter, cut bread into four inch circles, or to fit your breakfast sandwich maker. Spread spicy brown mustard over one side of both slices of bread.
4. Place one slice of bread into the bottom bread well, mustard side up. Top with sliced Provolone.
5. Lower cooking plate and top ring. Fill with seasoned roast beef and top with roasted red peppers. Cover with second slice of Rye bread, mustard side down.
6. Cover and set your timer for five minutes.
7. Before opening, slide out the cooking plate. Then lift the cover and top ring.
8. Remove, serve, and enjoy!

South African Gatsby on a French Baguette

Instructions:

1. Make sure your breakfast sandwich maker is turned on and preheating.
2. In a bowl, combine all seasonings and rub over sliced or shaved steak. Set aside.
3. Lift cover, top ring, and cooking plate. Place lower half of the baguette into the bottom bread well. Top with sliced Cheddar, onion, tomato, and French fries.
4. Lower cooking plate and top ring. Fill with steak and top with tomato sauce. Cover with upper half of the French baguette.
5. Cover and set your timer for five minutes.
6. Before opening, slide out the cooking plate. Then lift the cover and top ring.
7. Remove, serve, and enjoy!

Ingredients:

- 2 oz. of sliced or shaved steak
- 1 thin slice of onion
- 1 thin slice of tomato
- Dash of garlic salt
- Dash of cumin
- Dash of curry powder
- Dash of crushed red pepper
- 1 tbsp. of tomato sauce
- ¼ cup of pre-cooked french fries (warmed or room temperature)
- 2-¼ in. sliced CHeddar cheese
- ½ of a French baguette (or cut to fit bread well), halved (toasted or room temperature)

VIII. INTERNATIONAL SANDWICHES

Austrian Bosna Wurst on a Kaiser Roll

Ingredients:

½ pre-cooked bratwurst, halved vertically

¼ in. slice of onion

1 tsp. of curry powder

2 tbsp. of Dijon mustard

1 Kaiser roll (toasted or room temperature)

Instructions:

1. Make sure your breakfast sandwich maker is turned on and preheating.
2. In a bowl, combine curry powder and Dijon mustard. Spread over both halves of the roll.
3. Place lower half of roll into bottom bread well. Top with sliced onion.
4. Lower cooking plate and top ring. Fill with pre-cooked bratwurst and top with upper half of the Kaiser roll.
5. Cover and set your timer for five minutes.
6. Before opening, slide out the cooking plate. Then lift the cover and top ring.
7. Remove, serve, and enjoy!

Malaysian Roti John on a French Baguette

Substitute shaved steak or any other meaty leftovers, as well!

Instructions:

1. Make sure your breakfast sandwich maker is turned on and preheating.
2. In a pan, heat oil to a simmer. Then add onion, garlic, and green chili. Season with salt and pepper.
3. Lift cover, top ring, and cooking plate. Place bottom half of the French baguette into the bottom bread well. Top with (drained) sauteed veggies.
4. Lower cooking plate and top ring. Fill with sliced or shaved chicken breast and top with tomato sauce. Cover with upper half of the French baguette.
5. Cover and set your timer for five minutes.
6. Before opening, slide out the cooking plate. Then lift the cover and top ring.
7. Remove with a plastic spatula, serve, and enjoy!

Ingredients:

- 2 oz. of sliced chicken breast
- 2 tbsp. of minced onion
- 1 tbsp. of minced garlic
- 2 tbsp. of oil
- 1 green chili, sliced
- 2 tbsp. of tomato sauce
- ½ of a French baguette (or cut to fit bread well), halved (toasted or room temperature)
- Salt and pepper to taste

Finnish Porilainen on Sourdough

Ingredients:

½ pre-cooked bratwurst, halved vertically

¼ in. sliced fresh onion

2 tbsp. of ketchup

2 tbsp. of relish

¼ cup of fresh baby spinach

2 slices of Sourdough (toasted or room temperature)

Instructions:

1. Make sure your breakfast sandwich maker is turned on and preheating.
2. Gather spinach into a stack and roll into a tight tube. Cut into thick ribbons from right to left.
3. With a large cookie cutter, cut bread into four inch circles, or to fit your breakfast sandwich maker. Spread relish over one slice and ketchup over the second.
4. Lift cover, top ring, and cooking plate. Place one slice of bread, condiment side up, into the bottom bread well. Top with fresh onion.
5. Lower cooking plate and top ring. Fill with sliced bratwurst and top with fresh spinach ribbons. Top with second slice of bread, condiment side down.
6. Cover and set your timer for five minutes.
7. Before opening, slide out the cooking plate. Then lift the cover and top ring.
8. Remove, serve, and enjoy!

Trinidadian Chickpea Double on Pita (Vegetarian)

Instructions:

1. Make sure your breakfast sandwich maker is turned on and preheating.
2. In a pan, bring oil to a simmer. Add onion and cook until translucent. Then add garlic and curry powder, mixing well. Add 2 tbsp. of water and add chickpeas. Cover and set simmer for five minutes. Then add cumin, salt and pepper, and 2 tbsp. water again. Simmer until chickpeas are tender.
3. Lift cover, top ring, and cooking plate. Place one piece of pita into the bottom bread well. Top with sliced cucumber.
4. Lower cooking plate and top ring. Fill with chickpea mixture. Top with second piece of pita.
5. Cover and set your timer for five minutes.
6. Before opening, slide out the cooking plate. Then lift the cover and top ring.
7. Remove with a plastic spatula, serve, and enjoy!

Ingredients:

- 2 oz. of canned chickpeas, drained and rinsed
- 1 tbsp. of oil, or as needed
- 2 tbsp. of water
- ¼ of an onion, minced
- 1 tbsp. of garlic, minced
- 1 tsp. of curry powder
- Dash of cumin
- Salt and pepper to taste
- 3 slices of fresh cucumber
- 2 mini pita, or cut to fit bread well (toasted or room temperature)

VIII. INTERNATIONAL SANDWICHES

Vietnamese Bahn Mi on a French Baguette

A traditional Vietnamese favorite, the recipes vary in difficulty but this sandwich is a fun, veggie-filled, and delicious easy way to try for yourself!

Ingredients:

¼ cup of vinegar

2 tbsp. of water

2 tbsp. of sugar

1 tbsp. of minced carrot

2 tbsp. of minced onion

2 tbsp. of mayonnaise

3 slices of fresh cucumber

½ of a fresh or pickled jalapeno, sliced

2 oz. of shaved or sliced chicken breast

Garlic salt to taste

Black pepper to taste

½ of a French baguette, or cut to fit bread well (toasted or room temperature)

Instructions:

1. Make sure your breakfast sandwich maker is turned on and preheating.
2. In a pan, bring vinegar, water, and sugar to a boil until sugar is dissolved, about one minute.
3. In a bowl, combine carrot, onion, jalapeno. Pour vinegar solution over the vegetables and let sit to marinate for twenty-five to thirty minutes. Then drain excess vinegar.
4. Spread mayo over the lower half of the baguette. Place into the bottom bread well of the breakfast sandwich maker. Top with sliced cucumber and vegetables.
5. Lower cooking plate and top ring. Fill with chicken breast. Sprinkle with garlic salt and pepper. Top with upper half of the baguette.
6. Close the cover and set your timer for five minutes.
7. Before opening, slide out the cooking plate. Then lift the cover and top ring.
8. Remove, serve, and enjoy!

Irish Corned Beef Reuben on Rye

Get ready for St. Patrick's day with this classic Irish favorite!

Instructions:

1. Make sure your breakfast sandwich maker is turned on and preheating.
2. With a large cookie cutter, cut the Rye into four inch circles, or to fit your breakfast sandwich maker.
3. In a bowl, whisk together oil, vinegar, mustard, salt, and pepper. Spread over one slice of bread. Spread the Thousand Island over the second slice.
4. Lift cover, top ring, and cooking plate. Place one slice of bread, condiment side up, into the bottom bread well. Top with sliced cheese and sauerkraut.
5. Lower cooking plate and top ring. Fill with corned beef and top with second slice of bread, condiment side down.
6. Cover and set your timer for five minutes.
7. Before opening, slide out the cooking plate. Then lift the cover and top ring.
8. Remove with a plastic spatula, serve, and enjoy!

Ingredients:

- 2 oz. of corned beef
- 1 tsp. of oil
- ½ tsp. of balsamic vinegar
- ½ tsp. of spicy brown mustard
- Dash of salt
- Dash of pepper
- 2 tbsp. of Thousand Island dressing
- 2-¼ in. slices of Swiss cheese
- ¼ cup of sauerkraut
- 2 slices of Rye bread (toasted or room temperature)

IX. Kid-Friendly

Tuna Salad, Granny Smith Apple, & American Cheese on White

Instructions:

1. Make sure your breakfast sandwich maker is turned on and preheating.
2. In a bowl, combine (drained) tuna, celery, salt, pepper, and mayo and mix until well blended.
3. Gather spinach into a stack and roll into a tight tube. Cut into thick ribbons from right to left.
4. With a large cookie cutter, cut bread into four inch circles, or to fit your breakfast sandwich maker. Place one slice of bread into the bottom bread well and top with American cheese and sliced apple.
5. Lower cooking plate and top ring. Fill with fresh tuna salad and top with spinach ribbons. Top with second slice of bread.
6. Cover and set your timer for five minutes.
7. Before opening, slide out the cooking plate. Then lift the cover and top ring.
8. Remove with a plastic spatula, serve, and enjoy!

Ingredients:

½ can of tuna

2 tbsp. of mayonnaise, or as needed

2 thick slices of Granny Smith apple

1 slice of American cheese

¼ cup of fresh baby spinach

1 tbsp. of chopped celery

2 slices of white bread (toasted or room temperature)

Salt and pepper to taste

Sloppy Joes with White Cheddar on a Hamburger Bun

IX. KID-FRIENDLY

Ingredients:

¼ cup of ground turkey

2 tbsp. of oil, or as needed

1 tbsp. of tomato paste

½ tbsp of brown sugar

2 tbsp. of diced tomato

2-¼ in. slices of white Cheddar cheese

1 hamburger bun, halved (toasted or room temperature)

Instructions:

1. Make sure your breakfast sandwich maker is turned on and preheating.

2. In a pan, bring oil to a simmer. Cook ground turkey until no longer pink, about five minutes. Then add tomato, tomato paste, and brown sugar and simmer for three-five minutes.

3. Place lower half of bun into the bottom bread well. Top with sliced Cheddar.

4. Lower cooking plate and top ring. Fill with turkey mixture. Top with upper half of the hamburger bun.

5. Cover and set your timer for three minutes.

6. Before opening, slide out the cooking plate. Then lift the cover and top ring.

7. Remove, serve, and enjoy!

Sliced Chicken Breast, Broccoli, & Cheddar on White

Instructions:

1. Make sure your breakfast sandwich maker is turned on and preheating.
2. With a large cookie cutter, cut bread into four inch circles, or to fit your breakfast sandwich maker.
3. In a bowl, combine pesto and mayo. Spread over both slices of bread.
4. Lift cover, top ring, and cooking plate. Place one slice of bread, condiment side up, into the bottom bread well. Top with sliced Cheddar and broccoli.
5. Lower cooking plate and top ring. Fill with chicken breast and season with salt and pepper to taste. Top with second slice of bread, mayo side down.
6. Cover and set your timer for five minutes.
7. Before opening, slide out the cooking plate. Then lift the cover and top ring.
8. Remove, serve, and enjoy!

Ingredients:

- 2 oz. shaved or sliced chicken breast
- ¼ cup of cooked broccoli, sliced
- 2-¼ in. slices of sharp Cheddar cheese
- 1 tsp. of basil pesto
- 2 tbsp. of mayo
- Salt and pepper to taste
- 2 slices of white bread (toasted or room temperature)

IX. KID-FRIENDLY

Roasted Turkey Breast, Marinara, & Mozzarella on a Hamburger Bun

Instructions:

1. Make sure your breakfast sandwich maker is turned on and preheating.
2. Place lower half of the bun into the bottom bread well. Top with sliced Mozzarella and pickle slices.
3. Lower cooking plate and top ring. Fill with turkey breast and top with marinara sauce. Cover with upper half of hamburger bun.
4. Cover and set your timer for five minutes.
5. Before opening, slide out the cooking plate. Then lift the cover and top ring.
6. Remove with a plastic spatula, serve, and enjoy!

Ingredients:

2 oz. of roasted sliced turkey breast

2 tbsp. of marinara sauce

2-¼ slices of Mozzarella cheese

3-4 slices of dill pickles

1 hamburger bun, halved (toasted or room temperature)

Sliced Apple, Bacon, Honey, Butter on a French Baguette

A sweet and crispy breakfast or after-school snack sandwich that kids with love!

Instructions:

1. Make sure your breakfast sandwich maker is turned on and preheating.
2. Spread butter and honey over both halves of the baguette. Place lower half of the baguette into the bottom bread well. Top with slices of apple.
3. Lower cooking plate and top ring. Fill with pre-cooked sliced bacon. Top with upper half of the bread.
4. Cover and set your timer for five minutes.
5. Before opening, slide out the cooking plate. Then lift the cover and top ring.
6. Remove, serve, and enjoy!

Ingredients:

- 2 slices of pre-cooked bacon, halved crosswise
- 2 thick slices of fresh red apple
- 2 tbsp. of honey
- 2 tbsp. of butter
- ½ of a French baguette

Crunch Peanut Butter, Strawberry, & Brie Biscuit Sandwich (Vegetarian)

IX. KID-FRIENDLY

Ingredients:

2 tbsp. of chunky peanut butter

¼ cup of fresh strawberries, sliced

2-¼ in. slices of Brie cheese

1 16-oz Pillsbury biscuit, halved (toasted or room temperature)

Instructions:

1. Make sure your breakfast sandwich maker is turned on and preheating.
2. Spread chunky peanut butter over both halves of sliced biscuit.
3. Lift cover, top ring, and cooking plate. Place one half, butter side up, into the bottom bread well. Top with sliced Brie.
4. Lower cooking plate and top ring. Fill with sliced strawberries and top with upper half of the biscuit.
5. Cover and set your timer for two minutes.
6. Before opening, slide out the cooking plate. Then lift the cover and top ring.
7. Remove, serve, and enjoy!

Honey-Glazed Ham, Grape Jelly, & Provolone Waffle Sandwich

Instructions:

1. Make sure your breakfast sandwich maker is turned on and preheating.
2. Spread a thin layer of jelly onto both waffles. Place one waffle into the bottom bread well. Top with sliced Provolone.
3. Lower cooking plate and top ring. Fill with sliced ham and top with second waffle, fruit side down.
4. Cover and set your timer for two minutes.
5. Before opening, slide out the cooking plate. Then lift the cover and top ring.
6. Remove, serve, and enjoy!

Ingredients:

- 2 oz. of sliced honey-glazed ham
- 2 tbsp. of grape jelly
- 2-¼ in. slices of Provolone cheese
- 2 pre-cooked frozen waffles (toasted or room temperature)

Classic Peanut Butter & Jelly Bagel Sandwich (Vegan)

Ingredients:

2 tbsp. (vegan) peanut butter

2 tbsp. of grape jelly

1 bagel, halved (toasted or room temperature)

Instructions:

1. Make sure your breakfast sandwich maker is turned on and preheating.
2. Spread peanut butter over one half of the bagel and the jelly over the second half.
3. Place one half the the bagel into the bottom bread well Slide out cooking plate and lower top ring. Fill with second bagel half.
4. Cover and set your timer for one minute.
5. Remove, serve, and enjoy!

Cheddar, American, & Pickles Grilled Cheese on Wheat (Vegetarian)

Instructions:

1. Make sure your breakfast sandwich maker is turned on and preheating.

2. With a large cookie cutter, cut bread into four inch circles, or to fit your breakfast sandwich maker. Spread butter over one side over both slices of bread.

3. Lift cover, top ring, and cooking plate. Place one slice of bread, butter side down, into the bottom bread well. Top with cheeses.

4. Lower cooking plate and top ring. Fill with sliced pickles. Top with second slice of bread.

5. Close the cover and set your timer for three minutes.

6. Before opening, slide out the cooking plate. Then lift the cover and top ring.

7. Remove with a plastic spatula, serve, and enjoy!

Ingredients:

2-¼ in. slices of Cheddar cheese

1 slice of American cheese

2 tbsp of butter

4-5 slices of dill pickles

2 slices of wheat bread (toasted or room temperature)

Fruity Chicken Salad & Potato Chips on White

IX. KID-FRIENDLY

Ingredients:

½ can of chicken

2 tbsp. of mayonnaise, or as needed

1 slice of American cheese

¼ cup of diced grapes

¼ cup of potato chips

2 slices of white bread (toasted or room temperature)

Instructions:

1. Make sure your breakfast sandwich maker is turned on and preheating.
2. In a bowl, combine mayo and canned chicken. Mix until smooth. Add grapes and stir.
3. With a large cookie cutter, cut bread into four inch circles, or to fit your breakfast sandwich maker. Place one slice of bread into the bottom bread well. Top with American cheese.
4. Lower cooking plate and top ring. Fill with chicken salad and top with arugula. Cover with second slice of bread.
5. Cover and set your timer for two minutes.
6. Before opening, slide out the cooking plate. Then lift the cover and top ring.
7. Remove with a plastic spatula, serve, and enjoy!

X. Brunch

Caramelized Apple, Brie, & Bacon on Sourdough

Ingredients:

3 slices of fresh red apple

2-¼ in. slices of Brie

3 tbsp. of butter

1 tbsp. of sugar

2 tsp of heavy cream

2 slices of pre-cooked bacon, halved crosswise

2 slices of Sourdough bread (toasted or room temperature)

Instructions:

1. Make sure your breakfast sandwich maker is turned on and preheating.

2. In a pan, bring butter to a simmer and sprinkle with sugar. Stir for one minute, or until sugar begins to melt Add apples and saute until apples are a tender brown. Stir in cream and simmer for five minutes.

3. With a large cookie cutter, cut bread into four inch circles, or to fit your breakfast sandwich maker. Place one slice of bread into the bottom bread well. Top with sliced Brie.

4. Lower cooking plate and top ring. Fill well with caramelized apples. Top with second slice of bread.

5. Cover and set your timer for five minutes.

6. Before opening, slide out the cooking plate. Then lift the cover and top ring.

7. Remove, serve, and enjoy!

Maple Sausage, Strawberry Jam, & Nutella French Toast Sandwich

Instructions:

1. Make sure your breakfast sandwich maker is turned on and preheating.
2. Spread jam over one slice of French toast and Nutella over the other.
3. Lift cover, top ring, and cooking plate. Place one slice of bread, condiment side up, into the bottom bread well.
4. Lower cooking plate and top ring. Fill with pre-cooked maple sausage patty. Top with second slice of bread.
5. Cover and set your timer for five minutes.
6. Before opening, slide out the cooking plate. Then lift the cover and top ring.
7. Remove, serve, and enjoy with maple syrup for dipping.

Ingredients:

- 2 oz. pre-cooked maple sausage (heated to at least 40 degrees)
- 2 tbsp. of strawberry jam
- 2 tbsp. of Nutella
- ¼ cup of warmed maple syrup
- 2 slices of pre-cooked French toast (toasted or room temperature)

Caramelized Pear, Berry Cream Cheese, and Honey-Glazed Ham French Toast Sandwich

Ingredients:

2 oz. of sliced honey-glazed ham

3 tbsp. of cream cheese

1 tbsp of berry jam

3 slices of fresh pear

3 tbsp. of butter

1 tbsp. of sugar

2 tsp of heavy cream

2 slices of pre-cooked French toast (toasted or room temperature)

¼ cup of warmed maple syrup

Instructions:

1. Make sure your breakfast sandwich maker is turned on and preheating.

2. In a pan, bring butter to a simmer and sprinkle with sugar. Stir for one minute, or until sugar begins to melt. Add pears and saute until pears are a tender brown. Stir in cream and simmer for five minutes.

3. With a large cookie cutter, cut bread into four inch circles, or to fit your breakfast sandwich maker.

4. In a bowl, combine cream cheese and berry jam until well blended. Spread over both slices of bread. Place one slice of bread into the bottom bread well, cream cheese side up.

5. Lower cooking plate and top ring. Fill with caramelized pear and top with sliced ham. Cover with second slice of French toast, cream cheese side down.

6. Cover and set your timer for five minutes.

7. Before opening, slide out the cooking plate. Then lift the cover and top ring.

8. Remove, serve, and enjoy with warmed maple syrup for dipping.

Sliced Chicken Breast, Goat Cheese, & Raspberry Jam English Muffin Sandwich

Instructions:

1. Make sure your breakfast sandwich maker is turned on and preheating.
2. Spread jam over both sliced halves of the muffin. Place lower half of the muffin into the bottom bread well. Top with crumbled Goat cheese.
3. Lower cooking plate and top ring. Fill with chicken breast. Top with upper half of the English muffin, fruit side down.
4. Cover and set your timer for three minutes.
5. Before opening, slide out the cooking plate. Then lift the cover and top ring.
6. Remove with a plastic spatula, serve, and enjoy!

Ingredients:

- 2 oz. of sliced or shaved chicken breast
- 2 tbsp. of crumbled Goat cheese
- 3 tbsp. of raspberry jam
- 1 English muffin, halved (toasted or room temperature)

X. BRUNCH

Caprese Waffle Sandwich with Sweet Balsamic Glaze (Vegetarian)

Ingredients:

2-¼ in. slices of Mozzarella cheese

3-¼ in. slices of fresh tomato

2 fresh basil leaves

1 tbsp. of balsamic glaze

2 pre-cooked frozen waffles (toasted or room temperature)

Instructions:

1. Make sure your breakfast sandwich maker is turned on and preheating.

2. Lift cover, top ring, and cooking plate. Place one waffle into the bottom bread well. Top with sliced Mozzarella.

3. Lower cooking plate and top ring. Fill well with sliced tomato. Drizzle balsamic glaze over the slices. Top with second waffle.

4. Close the cover and set your timer for three minutes.

5. Before opening, slide out the cooking plate. Then lift the cover and top ring.

6. Remove, serve, and enjoy!

Sweet Lemon Cream Cheese and Fresh Berry Waffle Sandwich (Vegetarian)

Instructions:

1. Make sure your breakfast sandwich maker is turned on and preheating.
2. In a bowl, combine honey, lemon juice, and cream cheese. Spread over one waffle. Spread lemon curd over the second waffle.
3. Place one waffle into the bottom bread well, topping side up.
4. Lower cooking plate and top ring. Fill well with fresh berries and top with second waffle, topping side down.
5. Cover and set your timer for five minutes.
6. Before opening, slide out the cooking plate. Then lift the cover and top ring.
7. Remove, serve, and enjoy!

Ingredients:

- 2 tbsp. of cream cheese
- 1 tsp. of fresh lemon juice
- 2 tsp. of honey
- 2 tbsp. of lemon curd
- ¼ cup of fresh berries of your choice
- 2 pre-cooked frozen waffles (toasted or room temperature)

Monte Cristo French Toast Sandwich with Fresh Strawberries

Ingredients:

2 oz. of sliced smoked ham

2-¼ in. slices of Gruyere cheese

2 tbsp. of fresh strawberries, sliced

2 tbsp. of butter

¼ cup of warmed maple syrup

2 slices of pre-cooked French toast (toasted or room temperature)

1 tsp. of powdered sugar

Instructions:

1. Make sure your breakfast sandwich maker is turned on and preheating.

2. With a large cookie cutter, cut bread into four inch circles, or to fit your breakfast sandwich maker. Spread butter on side of each slice. Place on slice into the bottom bread well, butter side down. Top with sliced Gruyere and fresh strawberries.

3. Lower cooking plate and top ring. Fill with sliced smoked ham. Top with second slice of the French toast, butter side up.

4. Cover and set your timer for five minutes.

5. Before opening, slide out the cooking plate. Then lift the cover and top ring.

6. Remove, serve, and enjoy with warmed maple syrup for dipping!

XI. Breakfast Sides

Simple Roasted Breakfast Potatoes

(Two servings)

Ingredients:

1 red skinned potato, finely diced

3 tbsp. of diced bell pepper

2 tbsp. of diced onion

2 tbsp. of butter

Dash of garlic powder

Salt and pepper to taste

Instructions:

1. In a pan, combine butter, potato, and vegetables and cook at a medium heat. Season with salt, pepper, and garlic salt.

2. Saute until potatoes are tender. Turn up heat to high for one minute to make potatoes extra crispy.

3. Serve with ketchup or over eggs.

Simple Hash Brown "Casserole"

(Two servings)

Instructions:

1. Make sure your breakfast sandwich maker is turned on and preheating.
2. Spray the bottom bread well of the machine with non-stick oil of the surface and sides. Fill with half a cup of hash browns. Top with shredded cheese and season with salt and pepper to taste.
3. Lower cooking plate and top ring. Spray surface and sides with non-stick oil and fill well with the second half-cup of hash browns.
4. Cover and set your timer for five-ten minutes.
5. Before opening, slide out the cooking plate. Then lift the cover and top ring.
6. Remove, serve, and enjoy!

Ingredients:

- 1 cup of hash browns
- ⅓ cup of heavy cream
- ¼ cup of shredded Cheddar cheese
- Non-stick cooking spray
- Salt and pepper to taste

Savory Sauteed Brussel Sprouts & Bacon

(Two servings)

Ingredients:

1 cup of tripped brussel sprouts

2 strips of pre-cooked bacon

1 tbsp. of butter

1 tsp. of minced garlic

2 tsp. of balsamic vinegar

Instructions:

1. Chip bacon into thin strips.
2. In a pan, bring butter to a simmer. Add brussel sprouts and lightly fry eight to nine minutes. Then add garlic and balsamic vinegar and saute for one more minute.
3. Serve and enjoy!

XI. BREAKFAST SIDES

Citrus & Avocado Arugula Salad

(One serving)

Instructions:

1. In a bowl, cut out segments of grapefruit and orange and squeeze out excess juice. Place over fresh arugula. Drizzle with oil and sprinkle with salt and pepper to taste.
2. Serve and enjoy!

Ingredients:

3 oz. of fresh arugula

1 avocado, diced

1 grapefruit

1 orange

1 tbsp. of oil

Salt and pepper to taste

XI. BREAKFAST SIDES

Simple Potato Latkes

(One-two servings)

Ingredients:

1 cup of grated potato

¼ cup of onion, grated

1 egg

1 tsp. of flour

2 tbsp. of oil, or as needed

Salt and pepper to taste

Instructions:

1. Combine potato, onion, and salt and pepper. Divide into two parts and place both parts onto a paper towel. Lift corners and squeeze out excess liquid.

2. Place back into bowl and add egg, flour, and more salt and pepper to taste.

3. Divide potato mixture into three potato patties.

4. In a pan, bring oil to a simmer. Add potato latkes and fry on both sides for three to four minutes or until golden brown.

5. Serve and enjoy.

Sauteed Green Beans with Bacon & Onion

(Two servings)

Instructions:

1. Chop bacon into thin strips.
2. In a pan, bring oil to a simmer. Add green beans and onion and fry lightly for three to five minutes.
3. Top with crumbled Goat cheese and season with garlic salt and pepper to taste.
4. Serve and enjoy!

Ingredients:

- 1 cup of steamed or boiled green beans
- 2 strips of pre-cooked bacon
- ¼ cup of onion, diced
- 2 tbsp. of Goat cheese
- 2 tbsp. of oil, or as needed
- Garlic salt to taste
- Black pepper to taste

Classic Pan-Fried Home Fries

(Two servings)

Ingredients:

1 boiled potato, cut into wedges

2 tbsp. of oil, or as need

¼ cup of onion, diced

Salt and pepper to taste

Instructions:

1. In a pan, bring oil to a simmer. Add onion and cook until translucent, about five minutes.

2. Add potato and cook, turning wedges, for about fifteen minutes, or until crispy. Season with salt and pepper to taste.

Citrus, Honey, and Toasted Coconut Salad

(One serving)

Instructions:

1. Arrange sliced citrus in a bowl or plate. Top with sunflower seeds and coconut. Drizzle with honey.
2. Serve and enjoy!

Ingredients:

1 grapefruit, peeled and sliced

2 clementines, peeled and sliced

¼ cup roasted sunflower seeds

¼ toasted and shaved coconut

2 tbsp. of honey

Super Simple Frozen Fruit Salad

(Serves two)

Ingredients:

1 cup of grapes, halved

1 cup of strawberries, sliced

1 banana, ¼ in. sliced

Instructions:

1. Arrange fruit across a small pan and freeze for one hour.
2. Arrange into bowls and serve.

XII. Dessert

Fresh Strawberry, Banana, and Nutella Waffle Sandwich

XII. DESSERT

Ingredients:

2 tbsp. of Nutella

¼ cup of fresh strawberries, sliced

1 banana, ¼ in. sliced

1 cup of your choice of ice cream

2 pre-cooked frozen waffles (toasted or room temperature)

Instructions:

1. Make sure your breakfast sandwich maker is turned on and preheating.
2. Spread Nutella over both waffles.
3. Lift cover, top ring, and cooking plate. Place one waffle, spread side up, into the bottom bread well. Top with sliced strawberries.
4. Lower cooking plate and top ring. Top with sliced banana and cover with second waffle, spread side down.
5. Cover and set your timer for two minutes.
6. Before opening, slide out the cooking plate. Then lift the cover and top ring.
7. Cut sandwich into quarters and serve with your choice of ice cream!

Dark Chocolate 'S'mores Cinnamon Swirl Sandwich

Instructions:

1. Make sure your breakfast sandwich maker is turned on and preheating.
2. With a large cookie cutter, cut bread into four inch circles, or to fit your breakfast sandwich maker.
3. In a bowl, combine butter, graham cracker crumbs, and sugar until well blended
4. Spread butter mixture on one side of both slices of bread. Spread Nutella one the other side of one slice and marshmallow cream on the other side of the second slice.
5. Lift cover, top ring, and cooking plate. Place one slice of bread, condiment side up and butter side down, into the bottom bread well. Top with chocolate bar.
6. Slide out cooking plate and lower top ring. Fill with second waffle, butter side up.
7. Cover and set your timer for five minutes.
8. Before opening, slide out the cooking plate. Then lift the cover and top ring.
9. Remove and cut into quarters. Enjoy over your favorite ice cream!

Ingredients:

- 1 tbsp. of butter
- 2 tbsp. of graham cracker crumbs
- 1 tsp of sugar
- 2 slices of cinnamon swirl bread (toasted or room temperature)
- 2 tbsp. of Nutella
- ½ of a dark chocolate bar
- 1 cup of your choice of ice cream
- 2 tbsp. whipped marshmallow cream

XII. DESSERT

Peanut Butter, Bacon, & Dark Chocolate Croissant Sandwich

Ingredients:

2 tbsp. of crunchy peanut butter

2 strips of pre-cooked bacon, halved crosswise

½ dark chocolate bar

1 croissant, halved (toasted or room temperature)

Instructions:

1. Make sure your breakfast sandwich maker is turned on and preheating.
2. Spread peanut butter over the lower half of the croissant. Place into the bottom bread well. Top with dark chocolate.
3. Lower cooking plate and top ring. Fill with bacon and top with upper half of croissant.
4. Cover and set your timer for two minutes.
5. Before opening, slide out the cooking plate. Then lift the cover and top ring.
6. Remove and cut into quarters. Serve over your favorite choice of ice cream!

Granny Smith Apple & Honey Goat Cheese on Sugar-Encrusted Cinnamon Raisin Bread

Instructions:

1. Make sure your breakfast sandwich maker is turned on and preheating.
2. In a bowl, combine butter and sugar. Spread over one side of both slices of bread. Place one slice of bread into the bottom bread well, butter side down. Top with sliced cheese.
3. Lower cooking plate and top ring. Fill with sliced apple and drizzle with honey. Top with second slice of bread, butter side up.
4. Cover and set your timer for two minutes.
5. Before opening, slide out the cooking plate. Then lift the cover and top ring.
6. Remove and cut into quarters. Serve with your favorite ice cream!

Ingredients:

- 2-¼ in. slices of Mascarpone cheese
- 1 tbsp. of honey
- 1 tbsp. of butter
- 1 tsp. of sugar
- ½ of a Granny Smith apple, thinly sliced
- 2 slices of cinnamon raisin bread (toasted or room temperature)
- 1 cup of your choice of ice cream

XII. DESSERT

Chocolate & Brie Melt on Sourdough

Ingredients:

3-¼ in. slices of Brie cheese

½ of a milk chocolate bar

2 slices of Sourdough bread

1 tbsp. of butter, softened

Instructions:

1. Make sure your breakfast sandwich maker is turned on and preheating.
2. With a large cookie cutter, cut bread into four inch circles, or to fit your breakfast sandwich maker. Spread butter over one side of both slices of bread.
3. Lift cover, top ring, and cooking plate. Place one slice of bread, butter side down, into the bottom bread well. Top with sliced cheese and milk chocolate.
4. Slide out the cooking plate and lower the top ring. Fill well with second slice of bread, butter side up.
5. Cover and set your timer for five minutes.
6. Lift the cover and top ring.
7. Remove with a plastic spatula, serve, and enjoy!

Bacon, Banana, & Nutella on Sugar-Encrusted Cinnamon Raisin Bread

Instructions:

1. Make sure your breakfast sandwich maker is turned on and preheating.
2. With a large cookie cutter, cut bread into four inch circles, or to fit your breakfast sandwich make.
3. In a bowl, combine sugar and butter and blend until mixed. Spread over one side of both slices of bread. Spread Nutella over one slice of bread.
4. Place one slice of bread into the bottom bread well, butter side down and plain side up. Top with sliced bacon.
5. Lower cooking plate and top ring. Fill with sliced banana and top with the second slice of bread, Nutella side down and butter side up.
6. Cover and set your timer for two minutes.
7. Before opening, slide out the cooking plate. Then lift the cover and top ring.
8. Remove and cut into quarters. Serve with your choice of ice cream!

Ingredients:

- 2 slices of pre-cooked bacon, halved crosswise
- 1 tbsp. of butter
- 1 tsp. of sugar
- 2 tbsp. of Nutella
- 1 banana, ¼ in. sliced
- 2 slices of cinnamon raisin bread (toasted or room temperature)
- 1 cup of your choice of ice cream

XII. DESSERT

It's a fact: readers who follow an ACTION GUIDE as they read and use cookbooks tend to have the most success!

Here's what I'm going to do to thank you for downloading my book. Go to the link below to instantly sign up for these bonuses.

Here's just a taste of what subscribers get:

Printable Kitchen Guides:

- Keep your food fresher for longer with the Extra-Long Food Storage Guide
- No more guess work in the kitchen -- Metric Conversion Guide
- Make delicious spreads in minutes -- Easy Spreads Guide
- Protect your family from consuming undercooked meat -- Meat Grilling Guide
- Many more new upcoming high-quality guides

Books and Recipes:

- New mouth-watering recipes you have NEVER tried before
- New books I publish for FREE

GRAB YOUR FREEBIES NOW AT
COOKINGWITHAFOODIE.COM

Made in the USA
Middletown, DE
27 December 2019